T0335329

Election 2014

Election 2014

Why the Republicans Swept the Midterms

Ed Kilgore

PENN

UNIVERSITY OF PENNSYLVANIA PRESS

PHILADELPHIA

Published by
University of Pennsylvania Press
Philadelphia, Pennsylvania 19104–4112
www.upenn.edu/pennpress

Printed in the United States of America

A Cataloging-in-Publication record is
available from the Library of Congress

Cover design by John Hubbard

ISBN 978-0-8122-4744-2 hardcover
ISBN 978-0-8122-9166-7 ebook

For Dawn Wilson

Contents

P r e f a c e

"Campaign books" are a strange genre of American non-fiction, heavily influenced by a few models from the relatively recent past. There is most obviously the *Making of the President* series by Theodore White, covering the presidential elections from 1960 through 1972. (A final volume discussed the 1980 elections in the context of a revised take on the previous quarter century.) These books were self-consciously "official" in tone and relied heavily on authorized reporting of the major contenders, with most of the analysis focused on the winning campaign (as the titles suggested). Then there is the deliberately iconoclastic countermodel of "gonzo journalist" Hunter S. Thompson's *Fear and Loathing on the Campaign Trail 1972*, which abandoned objectivity and every other rule of conventional political reporting in the pursuit of "deeper truths" about American politics and government and an impressionistic presentation of the frenetic pace and sheer hellishness of a national campaign. A number of insider-outsider hybrid books have since occasionally appeared, the best received of which was Richard Ben Cramer's *What It Takes*, an account of the 1988 presidential campaign that owed a lot of its perspective to the fact that it was not published until 1992. The most recent exemplar in the field was probably *Game Change*, Mark Halperin and John Heilemann's book on the 2008 campaign that wrung a made-for-television movie out of its sensationalistic scoops and its focus on a single factor (the selection of Sarah Palin as John McCain's running mate) in a complicated election.

You will note that none of these books was about a midterm election, probably because midterm elections (with the possible exception of the 1994 contest, with its semimythical "Contract with America" and Newt Gingrich as a protagonist) typically lack the dominant personalities and clean story lines of presidential cycles. No, midterms have been largely left to the political scientists to dissect, beyond the rearview-mirror accounts prepared as background to the next batch of presidential campaign histories. This book seeks to break that mold by treating a midterm election as a unique event worth understanding.

While not strictly speaking a work of political science, this book does aim at providing a clear understanding of the dynamics of the 2014 elections that transcends (while often drawing upon) the episodic reporting and analysis of political journalists—and without the benefit of later hindsight. My own hybrid experience as a "news-cycle" blogger for *Washington Monthly* (writing twelve posts a day), a weekly columnist for *Talking Points Memo*, and the managing editor of an online forum focused on political strategy placed me in a position to think and write critically about the media coverage that shaped perceptions of the "midterms" even as they were unfolding. In that spirit, this book challenges questionable elements of the conventional wisdom surrounding the 2014 elections before it completely congeals.

I believe the trajectory and outcome of the 2014 midterms were relatively predictable and almost entirely explainable by a set of "fundamental" factors—including the electoral landscape, midterm turnout patterns, the president's approval ratings, sour perceptions of the economy and of politics, and some external news accidents—that all favored Republican candidates. It was in the continuing interest of both political journalists and partisan operatives, however, to give these fundamentals at most lip service while crafting dramatic narratives that credited the players in the electoral "game" with a lot more control over events than was justified. This endowed the elections themselves with more significance in signaling the future direction of American politics than we have good reason to assume. On the margins, of course, all sorts of factors, including dubious media narratives, affect electoral outcomes, so they, too, are part of our story.

I have sought in these pages to suspend my own political and ideological allegiances and dispassionately analyze what happened and why, and I apologize for any failures in achieving that posture. This was not, on balance, a particularly entertaining election cycle, and the daily grind of watching myriad candidates from each party hammer away monotonously on the same handful of cookie-cutter themes was not always an edifying experience. I hope to spare readers the tedium of following this election cycle and instead pare it down to its essential features, results, and implications. Those are interesting enough without the embellishments of imaginative journalists and ambitious spinners.

We obviously do not know at this point how history will regard the 2014 elections. As was the case after the 2010 elections, Republicans hope they have achieved a breakthrough that makes the presidency of Barack Obama a Waterloo for liberalism. Democrats just as naturally view this election as a cyclical setback at odds with their party's long-term advantages; some blame the president for the 2014 results and look forward to a post-Obama era. In this era of the "permanent campaign," we have already entered the 2016 campaign cycle. And each party's understanding—and misunderstanding—of what just happened may influence the next chapter of American political history.

Chapter 1

The Fundamentals and the Narrative

The midterm elections of 2014 were probably the most widely examined and debated of their kind in American history, and not because they were necessarily "historic" or even remarkable. This cycle did, however, coincide with a sudden upsurge in interest in the science of election analysis, some coming from political scientists entering the mainstream conversation in increasing numbers and some from journalists applying statistical methods popularized in other fields, including sports. Add in a continuation of the recent growth in publicly available polling data and an atmosphere of partisan and ideological polarization that has inevitably intensified all arguments over politics, and you have a cycle exhibiting a constant contrast between a "turned-off" electorate exhibiting disdain for both parties and for politics and government generally and highly engaged activists and pundits battling over interpretation of every development.

Midterm elections are often interpreted as interludes and prefaces, providing context and sometimes contrast to the better-known and more momentous presidential contests. But some, typically landslides, are remembered as initiating "eras" and creating "classes" of subsequently

Ed Kilgore

distinguished politicians. In all but a very few recent cases, midterms produce losses for the party controlling the White House (see Figure 1).

"Second-term midterms"—those occurring in a second presidential term—are especially notorious for signaling fatigue with the incumbent presidential party. Only once since the nineteenth century has the presidential party actually made gains in a second-term midterm

Figure 1. Midterm Losses for the Party Controlling the White House

Year	President	House	Senate	Governors
1938	Roosevelt	−71	−6	−9
1942	Roosevelt	−55	−9	−4
1946	Truman	−45	−12	−2
1950	Truman	−29	−6	−6
1954	Eisenhower	−18	−1	−8
1958	Eisenhower	−48	−13	−4
1962	Kennedy	−4	+3	−1
1966	Johnson	−47	−4	−8
1970	Nixon	−12	+2	−11
1974	Nixon/Ford	−48	−5	5
1978	Carter	−15	−3	−5
1982	Reagan	−26	+1	−7
1986	Reagan	−5	−8	+8
1990	G. H. Bush	−8	−1	−1
1994	Clinton	−52	−8	−10
1998	Clinton	+5	0	0
2002	G. W. Bush	+8	+2	0
2006	G. W. Bush	−30	−6	−6
2010	Obama	−63	−6	−6
2014	Obama	−12	−8	−3

Sources: American Presidency Project, UC Santa Barbara, and National Governors Association.

(1998, an event so shocking that it led to the resignation of House Speaker Newt Gingrich). Meanwhile, 1938, 1950, 1958, 1966, 1974, 1986, and 2006 all produced large congressional and gubernatorial losses for the party controlling the White House (see Figure 2). In five of those seven cases (all but 1938 and 1986), poor midterm performance was a leading indicator of a presidential defeat in the ensuing cycle.

The high historical likelihood of second-term midterm losses for the presidential party has made this expectation part of what political scientists call the "fundamentals" that must be factored into any more ephemeral evaluation of what is happening during the campaign cycle (e.g., polls, campaign funding, and campaign "events").

A second fundamental thought to affect national election outcomes is the condition of the economy (or, in some models, voter perceptions of the economy), for which the

Figure 2. Second-Term Midterm Losses for the Party Controlling the White House

Year	President	Approval rating	House	Senate	Governors
1938	Roosevelt	60	−71	−6	−9
1950	Truman	41	−45	−12	−2
1958	Eisenhower	57	−48	−13	−4
1966	Johnson	44	−47	−4	−8
1974	Nixon/Ford	53	−48	−5	−5
1986	Reagan	64	−5	−8	+8
1998	Clinton	65	+5	0	0
2006	G. W. Bush	37	−30	−6	−6
2014	Obama	41	−12	−8	−3

Sources: American Presidency Project, UC Santa Barbara, and National Governors Association.

presidential incumbent party is held especially responsible. While the Great Recession that began in December 2007 and intensified in late 2008 officially ended in June 2009,[1] public perceptions of the economy remained sour in subsequent months and years, and even in 2014, when monthly employment reports showed mostly robust net gains and a slow but steady drop in the official unemployment rate, public perceptions of the economy and its likely future trajectory improved barely if at all.

A third fundamental is the exposure of the two parties to losses in particular categories of contests. Congressional seats (or governorships or state legislative chambers) in places where a party has shown unusual recent strength are especially "exposed," and recent landslides often produce "overexposure." Thus Democrats were vastly exposed to House losses in 2010 after winning two straight landslides in 2006 and 2008, and indeed they lost sixty-four seats. Republican control of the decennial redistricting process in many key states, along with superior "efficiency" in the distribution of Republican voters, reduced the GOP's exposure to losses in 2012; Democrats won only 201 of 435 seats despite winning the national House popular vote by more than a percentage point. Going into 2014, the general expectation was that the probable House outcomes ranged from small Democratic gains to small Republican gains, with the latter significantly more likely according to historical precedents. Meanwhile the Senate landscape could not have been much more positive for Republicans, with a "class" of senators representing a relatively low-population and nonurban range of states,[2] compounded by the exposure of Democratic senators elected or reelected in the very good Democratic election year of

2008, along with the retirements of three veteran senators in Republican-leaning states (Max Baucus of Montana, Tim Johnson of South Dakota, and Jay Rockefeller of West Virginia). Ultimately Democrats were defending twenty-one of thirty-six seats at stake in 2014, including seven in states carried by Mitt Romney in 2012 (see Figure 3).

A fourth fundamental is the president's job approval rating; one reason second-term midterms usually cut against incumbents is that they rarely survive two terms with strong approval ratings. Indeed, the one modern exception to the pattern of second-term midterms costing the party controlling the White House seats in Congress occurred in 1998, when Bill Clinton's party was buoyed by both a booming economy and robust job approval ratings for the president (66 percent at the time of the 1998 elections).[3]

Senate Landscape in 2014

● Dem Inc./Carried by Obama '12   ⦂ GOP Inc./Carried by Obama '12
▓ GOP Inc./Carried by Romney '12   ⦂ Dem Open/Carried by Romney '12
░ Dem Inc./Carried by Romney '12   ⁄⁄ GOP Open/Carried by Romney '12

Figure 3. Senate Seats on the 2014 Ballot

Finally, a fifth fundamental is voter turnout patterns, which in midterms, for a variety of reasons, tend to produce an electorate that is smaller, older, and less diverse than in presidential elections. As noted at some length below, long-standing demographic patterns of participation and non-participation in nonpresidential elections have taken on an especially partisan dimension after 2006, producing what some have called a "two electorates" phenomenon.

Beyond the "fundamentals" is the vast number of factors that make up most of what political journalists, pundits, and partisan spinmeisters usually talk about in the course of an election cycle. Candidate quality, party resources, money, strategy and tactics, issue contrasts, campaign events or "moments," and such dubious, elusive assets as "momentum" and "enthusiasm" play a role that varies (depending on the observer) from nil (the view of some political scientists) to everything (as reflected in what might be called the *Game Change* school of political journalism, to use the title of the best-selling and seemingly made-for-HBO book about the 2008 presidential campaign). But even the latter camp, which often presumes that election outcomes are determined by a candidate's turn of a phrase, typically relies on deductive "narratives" that tie together diverse phenomena, with a greater or lesser fidelity to facts.

Because media "narratives" unarguably affect coverage and arguably also affect voter perceptions (sometimes after being adopted by candidates or their partisan allies), it's important to understand the major themes that the political commentariat carried into the midterm elections.

The twin events that dominated political coverage in the run-up to 2014 are clear enough: the government shutdown crisis of October 2013 and the botched rollout of the federal government's enrollment system for individual private insurance under the Affordable Care Act of 2010 (popularly known as Obamacare).

The government shutdown followed an extended period of escalating threats from congressional Republicans making demands—centered on but not confined to Obamacare—linked to a refusal to extend appropriations or approve a required debt limit increase. Many supporters of a deliberate shutdown strategy (or at least those with a willingness to risk one) were conservatives dissatisfied with the "surrender" of their leaders that ended the fiscal standoff of April 2011. Others were focused on blocking the implementation of the Affordable Care Act before or soon after the beginning of its open-enrollment period, which happened to coincide with the beginning of a new fiscal year at the beginning of October. As Speaker Boehner was gradually pushed into a confrontation with Senate Democrats and the White House he clearly did not relish, a one-year delay in the implementation of Obamacare became the key demand, with—or so it was rumored—smaller Obamacare concessions being treated as an acceptable fallback and trophy. The government duly shut down unessential operations, indefinitely furloughing about 800,000 federal employees, on October 1. Subsequent Republican efforts to blame the shutdown on Obama because he would not accept an omnibus appropriations bill that funded "everything but Obamacare" did not move public opinion.

In the end, a combination of the public's dissatisfaction with the shutdown and with the Republican Party and the business community's impatience over the risk of a debt default trumped conservative brinkmanship, and the shutdown ended after sixteen days. (John Boehner violated the so-called Hastert Rule, holding that no bill without support of a majority of Republican members should come to the House floor, and passed a Senate-passed bill temporarily extending the debt limit and appropriations with mostly Democratic votes.)

Luckily for Republicans, though, this rout coincided with a universally deplored rollout of Healthcare.gov, the portal created by the US Department of Health and Human Services as a central information point and purchasing platform for individual health insurance in the thirty-six states that did not create their own insurance exchanges.

As soon as the government shutdown ended on October 16, attention quickly shifted to problems with the Obamacare rollout. On October 21, the president was forced to make a speech from the Rose Garden addressing the website problems and explaining the enrollment process. On October 24 and again on October 31, Healthcare.gov crashed. On October 28, House Energy and Commerce Committee Chairman Fred Upton (R-MI) introduced legislation addressing rapidly escalating stories of individual health insurance policies being canceled. On October 30, the president had to hedge on his 2012 campaign statement that people happy with their health insurance plans could keep them. (They actually could not if the policies didn't comply with the minimum coverage requirements of the Affordable Care Act.) On October 31, Secretary of Human and Health Services Kathleen Sebelius referred to the enrollment launch as a "fiasco" and accepted responsibility.[4]

As the timeline suggests, Republicans were skillful in linking the technological meltdown of the site launch with other "Obamacare broken promises," notably the president's inadequately conditional assertion during the 2012 campaign that people happy with their health insurance could keep it. (Given the way individual health insurance works, that would not have been true even if the Affordable Care Act had never been enacted, but the minimum requirements for compliance with the new law guaranteed many cancellations.) More subtly, Republicans and the news media alike replaced talk of the Washington dysfunction symbolized by the government shutdown with Washington dysfunction symbolized by Healthcare.gov. Encouragingly for the GOP, the president's job approval rating (as measured by Gallup) sank below 40 percent in November for the first time since 2011.[5]

As the authoritative political observer Charlie Cook observed in December 2013, the impact of the shift in attention from the government shutdown to the Obamacare exchange rollout was even more dramatic in terms of the "generic congressional ballot" measuring party preferences in US House races:

> [When the shutdown began,] the Democratic numbers in the generic ballot began to pull dramatically ahead, resembling a steep ascent up the side of a mountain, ending about 7 points ahead of Republicans, 45 percent to 38 percent—an advantage that, were it to last until the election, would give Democrats a chance to recapture the House.
>
> Then, in mid-October, the focus shifted from the government-shutdown fiasco to a different debacle,

this time a Democratic disaster: the botched launch of the Obamacare website and subsequent implementation problems of the health care law, including termination notices going out to many people who had insurance coverage. The Democratic numbers from the generic-ballot test dropped from 45 percent to 37 percent, and Republicans moved up to 40 percent. This 10-point net shift from a Democratic advantage of 7 points to a GOP edge of 3 points in just over a month is breathtaking, perhaps an unprecedented swing in such a short period.[6]

It's certainly the case that any talk about a Democratic reconquest of the House, which spiked at the height of the government shutdown, all but ceased by the beginning of 2014.

Just as importantly, the sequence of events convinced many journalists and pundits that they had just witnessed the fault lines of the 2014 midterm elections, with the big questions being whether Republicans could restore their position as the "adult party" by fully reining in a newly chastened Tea Party faction and whether Democrats could repair or perhaps distance themselves from the Obama administration's "incompetence."

Subsequently, Republicans made it a major priority of 2014 to feed the dominant media narrative by constantly boasting of their new discipline and "pragmatism," as displayed both in the primaries and the general election campaign. Meanwhile, Democrats suffered from a long series of external events, mostly overseas and on the US-Mexico border, which in combination made it very difficult to project a confident and united party led by a competent president and administration. These events will be discussed in Chapter 3.

From the beginning, the marquee battle of the cycle was over control of the US Senate. Republicans felt they had missed opportunities to win the upper chamber in 2010 (when they gained six net seats) and in 2012 (when they actually lost two net seats), largely thanks to poor candidate quality and/or ideological extremism, depending on one's point of view.

In 2010, a seat in Delaware that Republican congressman Mike Castle was heavily favored to win went easily to Democrat Chris Coons after Castle lost a primary to a young and untested conservative named Christine O'Donnell, whose record of outlandish comments made her an immediate underdog. Similarly, the GOP thought it had Senate Majority Leader Harry Reid on the ropes in Nevada, but preferred Republican establishment candidate Sue Lowdon lost to Tea Party favorite Sharron Angle in the Republican primary and, like O'Donnell, succumbed to a pounding based on past extremist statements. And in Colorado, vulnerable incumbent Democrat Michael Bennet won a comeback victory attributable in no small part to questionable comments about women from GOP nominee Ken Buck, who seemed to epitomize the image of Republicans as cranky white men angry at the cultural changes of the previous half century.

In 2012, Republicans lost two Senate seats in deep-red states after the "wrong" candidate won primaries: in Indiana, where Richard Mourdock defeated longtime incumbent Richard Lugar and then lost to centrist Democrat Joe Donnelly, and in Missouri, where Todd Akin's campaign imploded after he made insensitive comments about rape in the course of defending an unpopular, absolute position on abortion.

As a result, in the early part of the 2014 cycle, both Republicans and the news media focused on the ability of the GOP to control its primaries and avoid the kind of upsets that produced weak nominees and party divisions in the previous two elections.

Some "victories" on this front occurred before the primaries, during the candidate recruitment phase of the cycle, most notably in Colorado, where failed 2010 GOP Senate nominee Ken Buck was running again. In February, a much more attractive and less gaffe-prone candidate, US Rep. Cory Gardner, announced his bid for the Senate, and Buck promptly dropped his own Senate bid to run instead for Gardner's open House seat.

Democrats had their own preoccupation entering the cycle—how to overcome an alignment of demographic groups that had suddenly given Republicans a significant advantage in midterms. Ron Brownstein summarized this development in a *National Journal* column as the campaign heated up:

> [W]hile the voting falloff between presidential-year and midterm elections has remained constant, its impact has been vastly magnified by a racial and generational realignment that has remade each party's base of support since the 1980s. In presidential and congressional races alike, Democrats today fare best among minorities, Millennials, and white voters (especially women) who are single or college-educated. Even in a country rapidly growing more diverse, Republicans still rely almost entirely on whites, running best

among those who are older, blue-collar, married, rural, and male. In other words, Democrats have become increasingly reliant on precisely the groups most likely to sit out midterms, while Republicans score best among those most likely to show up.[7]

Thus analysts have come to refer to "two electorates": one that is Democratic leaning and appears in presidential cycles; the other that is Republican leaning and appears in midterms. This change in the configuration of powers was most notable between the midterm elections of 2006 and 2010. In the former year, Democrats broke even among sixty-five-and-over voters (who represented 19 percent of the electorate), albeit narrowly. In 2010, Republicans won that demographic (which had risen to 21 percent of the electorate) by an astonishing twenty-one points. Figure 4 shows the oscillating nature of both participation and preference among key demographic groups from 2006 to 2014.

Figure 4. Democratic Share of the Vote in Selected Demographic Categories, 2006–2014 (percentage of total vote in parentheses)

Year	Whites	African Americans	Latinos	Under thirty	Sixty-five and over
2006	47 (79)	89 (10)	69 (8)	60 (12)	49 (19)
2008	43 (74)	95 (13)	67 (9)	66 (18)	45 (16)
2010	37 (77)	89 (11)	60 (8)	55 (12)	38 (21)
2012	39 (72)	93 (13)	71 (10)	60 (19)	44 (16)
2014	38 (75)	89 (12)	62 (9)	54 (13)	41 (22)

Source: CNN Exit Polls, 2006–2014.

Because of the special vulnerability of Democrats to Senate losses in 2014, it was the Democratic Senate Campaign Committee (DSCC) that most directly took on the task of changing midterm turnout patterns via an intensive use of the voter targeting and motivation techniques utilized so effectively by the Obama campaign in 2012.

In February 2014, Ashley Parker of the *New York Times* described this DSCC effort, dubbed the Bannock Street Project:

> The Democrats' plan to hold on to their narrow Senate majority goes by the name "Bannock Street project." It runs through 10 states, includes a $60 million investment and requires more than 4,000 paid staff members . . . [engaged in] an aggressive combination of voter registration, get-out-the-vote and persuasion efforts.
>
> They hope to make the 2014 midterm election more closely resemble a presidential election year, when more traditional Democratic constituencies— single women, minorities and young voters—turn out to vote in higher numbers . . .
>
> "Bannock Street" is drawn from the name of the Denver field headquarters for the campaign of Senator Michael Bennet, Democrat of Colorado. . . . Mr. Bennet won in 2010 in part by generating higher than forecast turnout.[8]

What endowed the Bannock Street Project with its special mystique was not, however, its evocation of a 2010 upset win but instead its incorporation of the Obama campaign's voter targeting and motivation techniques from 2012, which left a supposedly upgraded Republican GOTV (get-out-the-vote) effort in the distant dust.

Throughout the cycle, the Bannock Street Project appeared in media accounts of various races as a sort of will-o'-the-wisp, with a real presence via field offices opened and dollars spent but an entirely speculative impact; it was portrayed as a source of some magical thinking among Democrats who thought it was really possible to eliminate rather than mitigate "midterm fall-off" in pro-Democratic segments of the electorate.

While most of the attention of both parties was on the Senate landscape going into the cycle, there were, of course, House and state-level elections as well. As noted above, the limited "exposure" of both parties made a 2006- or 2010-style landslide in House races very unlikely. An April 2013 essay by the *Cook Political Report*'s David Wasserman, updating his organization's authoritative Partisan Voting Index ratings (a measurement of a district's relationship to the national average in the last two presidential elections), explained exactly how and why the House battleground had shrunk:

> The 2012 presidential results by district are remarkable in their own right: Republican presidential nominee Mitt Romney carried 226 districts to President Obama's 209, while losing the race by nearly four percent. This helps explain why House Democrats won 1.4 million more votes than House Republicans in 2012 but won just 201 of 435 seats. The House is well-sorted out: there are only 17 Republicans sitting in districts Obama carried, and only nine Democrats sitting in districts Romney carried.

This year's Partisan Voter Index illustrates how voters' geographical self-sorting, even more than redistricting, has driven the polarization of districts over the last decade. The 2012 round of redistricting diminished the number of "Swing Seats"—those with PVI scores between R+5 and D+5—from 103 to 99. But after the November 2012 election, the number of "Swing Seats" fell even more sharply, from 99 to 90. This means the number of competitive-range districts has fallen a total of 45 percent, from 164 to just 90, between 1998 and 2013.[9]

The shrinking number of competitive districts—and of Democratic opportunities for gains—was made even more apparent in Wasserman's House race ratings at the end of 2013: "Our newest House ratings count 43 competitive races in 25 Democratic-held and 18 GOP-held seats. But of the 25 Democratic seats, 10 are in the Toss Up column. Of the 18 GOP seats, just three are in the Toss Up column. If the election were held today, Democrats would need to win 42 of these 43 competitive races to win the House, a virtually impossible task."[10]

The massive Republican gubernatorial sweep of 2010 definitely limited opportunities for Republican gains and Democratic losses in 2014. Republicans were defending twenty-two governorships (eight in states carried by Obama in 2012) and Democrats only sixteen (just one in a state carried by Romney in 2012).

Chapter 2

The Primaries

The consensus that Tea Party candidates cost Republicans the Senate in 2010 and 2012 heavily influenced media coverage of the 2014 GOP Senate primaries, which was treated as an extended (and ultimately successful) effort by the Republican establishment to hold off another round of unhappy upsets.

Going into the cycle, there were distinctive, at least somewhat viable, Tea Party–oriented Senate candidates in Alaska (Joe Miller), Colorado (Ken Buck), Georgia (Paul Broun, Phil Gingrey, and Karen Handel), Iowa (Sam Clovis and Joni Ernst), Kansas (Milton Wolf), Kentucky (Matt Bevin), Nebraska (Ben Sasse), New Hampshire (Bob Smith), North Carolina (Greg Brannon and Mark Harris), and Texas (Steve Stockman).

Antennae were up for viable "constitutional conservative" challenges to two other theoretically vulnerable Republican incumbents: Lindsey Graham of South Carolina and Lamar Alexander of Tennessee. Through a combination of luck, close attention to the state, endorsements from prominent conservatives, and selective Obama bashing (particularly from Graham, who was Obama's shrillest foreign policy critic and a prime promoter of "Benghazi" conspiracy theories), both escaped viable primary opposition.

The first Senate primary, in Texas on March 4, was no contest, with Stockman running a largely invisible campaign against Cornyn. (Down-ballot, however, Lieutenant Governor David Dewhurst, fresh from losing a 2012 GOP Senate runoff to Ted Cruz, ran a poor second in his 2014 renomination bid to a fiery Tea Party state senator, Dan Patrick; Patrick won the runoff on May 27.)

In North Carolina on May 6, State House Speaker and establishment favorite Thom Tillis benefited from divided right-wing opposition, a 40 percent threshold to avoid a runoff, and a very conservative campaign message to win his state's Senate nomination.

On May 13 in Nebraska, Ben Sasse soundly defeated State Treasurer Shane Osborn (who actually finished third behind Sid Dinsdale) but only after the national GOP establishment began to claim Sasse, a former congressional staffer.

A week later the "GOP establishment quiets the Tea Party" meme probably peaked when Senate Minority Leader Mitch McConnell easily defeated Matt Bevin (after outspending him by at least three to one). The same day, Georgia's crowded GOP Senate field was topped by the two candidates least identified with the Tea Party— business executive David Perdue and US Rep. Jack Kingston, who qualified for a runoff. Early front-runners and "constitutional conservative" darlings Reps. Paul Broun Jr. and Phil Gingrey finished fourth and fifth.

But on June 3, the phenomenon that first occurred in Nebraska with the establishment adoption of Ben Sasse repeated itself in Iowa. Joni Ernst, a very conservative state senator with solid Tea Party / constitutional conservative credentials, managed to win endorsements from both Sarah Palin and Mitt Romney in March (whom she had endorsed for president in both 2008—when he was the "movement conservative" candidate—and 2012), just as she released the famed "Make 'em squeal" ad drawing on her upbringing on a hog farm where she claimed to have assisted in castrating the beasts (qualifying her to take on "pork," of course). Ernst also was the first Senate candidate to obtain backing from both the self-consciously right-wing Senate Conservatives Fund and the US Chamber of Commerce, an establishment stronghold.

The idea of a Tea Party/establishment "fusion," and/or an establishment cooptation of the conservative insurgency, gradually began to compete with the "triumph of the establishment" moderation as an interpretive framework for the cycle, though mostly in more conservative circles. It gained additional credence as the two establishment Senate candidates in Georgia, David Perdue and Jack Kingston, spent a long runoff campaign trying to turn each other's right flanks, with Perdue winning after an ad blitz attacking the US Chamber (which had strongly backed Kingston) for its support of immigration "amnesty."[1]

But the moment that most challenged the reigning "triumph of the establishment" narrative occurred outside the Senate battlefield, in a June 10 House primary in Virginia, where House Majority Leader and putative future Speaker Eric Cantor was beaten soundly by a nationally obscure economics professor named Dave Brat, mainly known for being simultaneously a conservative Christian and an acolyte of the atheist evangelist of laissez-faire capitalism, Ayn Rand. The repercussions were significant: Cantor was the heir apparent to Speaker John Boehner and also the most prominent political patron of a group of "reform conservatives" thought in some circles to represent the intellectual future of the GOP. Additionally, his defeat and subsequent resignation from the House deprived Republicans of their only non-Christian member of Congress.

Establishment jitters peaked in Mississippi and Kansas. Six-term incumbent Senator Thad Cochran of Mississippi was widely expected to retire in 2014 but chose instead to run for one more term at the age of seventy-six. Long a throwback to an older and more genteel style of southern Republicanism—reliably conservative on most issues but allergic to racial politics and very focused on delivering federal dollars to the state— Cochran had dodged major challenges for most of his career but finally ran out of luck. State senator Chris McDaniel, a former conservative talk radio host and a self-conscious Tea Party advocate, challenged Cochran with the closely related charges that the old senator had "gone native" in his many years in Washington and had perpetuated big government with his determination to bring home defense and nondefense bacon.

Cochran made a major mistake by listing a Washington address on his filing papers[2] for the election and initially ran a languid campaign short on personal appearances and relying on endorsements from the rest of the state's party establishment (most importantly former Gov. Haley Barbour and his brother Henry, a member of the Republican National Committee [RNC] and a hands-on advisor to Cochran). A strange incident captured

media attention for weeks: four men prominent in Mississippi Tea Party circles were caught trying to photograph
Rose Cochran, the senator's bed-ridden wife, in a Jackson
nursing home; they apparently wanted to use the "abandoned" wife as a metaphor for Cochran's "abandonment"
of Mississippi conservative values.

In the June 3 primary, McDaniel came breathtakingly
close to ending Cochran's Senate career; 4,854 votes for a
minor third candidate, Thomas Carey, kept the challenger
from achieving the majority necessary to avoid a runoff.
But given his momentum and the usually ideological
character of runoff voters, McDaniel was expected to win
the June 24 runoff.

In one of the very few examples in the entire cycle of
a Republican moving anywhere other than to the right to
head off a conservative primary challenge, Cochran's campaign (deploying a suddenly energized candidate) began
heavily emphasizing his value to Mississippi in bringing home federal projects and contracts (particularly in
the defense facilities of the Gulf Coast) and criticizing
McDaniel for disloyalty to Mississippi's needs and (usually through intermediaries) for racial insensitivity.[3] But
the most audacious tactic was the open targeting of African American voters—who in Mississippi nearly all vote
Democratic—who had not voted in the primary and thus
were eligible to "cross over" and support Cochran in the
runoff. (Democratic Party officials, sniffing the possibility of an unexpected competitive Senate race if McDaniel
was the nominee, discouraged "crossover" voting.)

Even a cursory analysis of voting patterns on runoff
night showed Cochran winning mainly on the strength
of relatively heavy turnout in areas with large African

American populations. Then and for weeks thereafter, McDaniel and his campaign fruitlessly sought through both legal and political channels to claim Cochran's "crossover" votes violated state law or unwritten Republican rules.[4]

Like Cochran, Kansas's Pat Roberts had a reputation as having "lost touch" with his state and was accused by intraparty critics of elevating special-interest "earmarks" above conservative resistance to big government. Challenged early on for not actually living in Kansas, Roberts incautiously joked he had "full access to the recliner" in a supporter's house and admitted his visits to the state tended to coincide with reelection campaigns.[5]

Luckily for Roberts, his Tea Party primary challenger, surgeon Milton Wolf, turned out to have bigger problems than the incumbent. Facebook posts showing him making irreverent comments about gruesome X-ray images of gunshot victims—recirculated happily by Roberts supporters—nearly killed his campaign and may well have kept him from victory.[6] Despite a general assumption that he would easily win, Roberts won the August 5 primary by just under seven points, with less than a majority.

The last chance for a Tea Party upset in Senate races was the August 19 primary in Alaska, a state where hyperconservative Joe Miller's upset win over Sen. Lisa Murkowski in a 2010 primary led to a rare, successful write-in campaign for the incumbent. With Miller running again in 2014 for the right to face Sen. Mark Begich, establishment Republicans began to coalesce around former Attorney General and Natural Resources Commissioner Dan Sullivan (as opposed to Lt. Gov. Mead Treadwell), a favorite of national GOP funding groups. Sullivan did win, but only after a surprising surge for Miller (who was calling for impeachment of the president) brought him within eight points of victory.[7]

One late primary that had an impact on the Senate without involving the possibility of a competitive general election contest was in Hawaii, where a complex struggle involving personal alliances and racial/ethnic loyalties broke out in the Democratic Party.

Just before longtime Sen. Daniel Inouye (a Japanese American) died in December 2012, he reportedly expressed the wish that he would be succeeded by US Rep. Colleen Hanabusa (also a Japanese American). But Gov. Neil Abercrombie (a *haole*, or white Hawaiian) instead appointed another *haole* (and his lieutenant governor) Brian Schatz to the position. While Schatz quickly became a favorite of progressives (and especially environmentalists) in Hawaii and nationally, Hanabusa challenged him in a special election to complete Inouye's term. Polling showed a very close race throughout; Schatz received a boost when Hawaii-native Barack Obama endorsed him, but his relationship with the increasingly unpopular Abercrombie and the strong likelihood of a heavy Asian vote for Hanabusa were problematic. On the eve of the August 9 primary, one tropical storm hit the islands and another approached. Schatz led Hanabusa very narrowly on primary day, but two precincts canceled voting due to flooded roads and an unusual delayed election was held for those locations the following Friday, with Schatz holding on for the win.[8]

The primaries had relatively little impact on prospects for either party in House races. Only five incumbents—four Republicans and one Democrat—lost in the primaries. Aside from Eric Cantor's shocking defeat—which didn't create an opening for Democrats but simply showed that the Tea Party was not necessarily the tamed beast the national narrative held it to be—none were significant nationally. A counterpoint to the Cantor primary was a May contest in Idaho, where the conservative Club for Growth targeted US Rep. Mike Simpson, hammering him in particular for supporting the Troubled Asset Relief Program (TARP) in 2008. Simpson won with more than 60 percent of the vote after a rescue mission by the US Chamber of Commerce and other probusiness groups.[9] Was this an example of the establishment taming the Tea Party and the GOP "moving to the center" or instead the GOP moving to the right to absorb an important faction while co-opting a challenge to the party leadership? That's a question that may not be answered until the presidential nominating contest of 2016.

Chapter 3

The General Election Campaign

As the general election campaign began to unfold in the early summer, the president's approval ratings in key Senate states were low: 38 percent in Arkansas, 45 percent in Colorado, 41 percent in Georgia, 40 percent in Iowa, 35 percent in Kansas, 33 percent in Kentucky, 35 percent in Louisiana, 39 percent in New Hampshire, and 41 percent in North Carolina. At roughly the same time, Democratic Senate candidates were at 45 percent in Arkansas, 45 percent in Kentucky, 44 percent in Colorado, 40 percent in Georgia, 45 percent in Kentucky, 41 percent in Louisiana, 49 percent in New Hampshire, and 41 percent in North Carolina.[1] For the most part, Democratic Senate candidates were outperforming the president, but in most of these contests, a high percentage of undecided voters appeared to give the president negative approval ratings.

The performance of the economy had generally improved during the first half of 2014, with strong GDP growth (4.6 percent) in the second quarter after a weather-affected dip in the first quarter[2] and with net job growth of over 1.3 million the first six months of the year.[3] But public perceptions of the economy had barely budged by the point in the summer when, according to research, voting preferences start to become fixed (and, even then, they are heavily colored by partisan affiliation, especially in midterms).

Building on the botched Obamacare enrollment launch, Republicans and pro-Republican groups decided to conduct an early and massive carpet bombing of Democrats, accentuating every negative perception and concern about the Affordable Care Act.

The conviction that Obamacare represented a major Democratic Achilles' heel—or perhaps simply an ideal topic for "energizing" the conservative "base"—led to some innovations in campaign advertising practices. Conservative groups, led by the Koch-affiliated Americans for Prosperity, ran an extraordinary number of early ads against Democrats in competitive races, attacking the health care law, as explained by *Bloomberg*'s Greg Giroux:

> More than 66,000 ads in U.S. House and Senate races aired through March 9, more than triple what candidates and allied groups aired during a comparable period four years ago, according to New York-based Kantar Media's CMAG, which tracks advertising.
>
> More than 30,000 of the ads had an anti-Obamacare message, a 12-fold increase from four years ago, according to data compiled by CMAG. The anti-Obamacare spots accounted for 45 percent of all ads, up from 12 percent during the comparable period leading up to the 2010 midterm elections.
>
> The findings also show the growing power of outside groups in attempting to influence elections. Organizations unaffiliated with any candidate account for 72 percent of ads for the 2014 campaign, compared with

13 percent in 2010, before changes to federal campaign-finance laws and regulations spurred the creation of some groups while increasing the clout of others.[4]

Meanwhile, as noted in Chapter 1, a series of external events shaped public perceptions of the contending forces in ways that almost uniformly reinforced Republican and media perceptions that the president and his party were incompetent managers of national security and/or were promoting policies bad for the country. The following is a brief account of how Obama's past politically salient accomplishments were neutralized or even reversed by the fast-moving events of 2014, as heavy mainstream media coverage of them coincided with Republican paid media efforts to disparage the administration and hold Democratic candidates responsible for its "failings."

From the Strategic Tilt to Asia to Putin's Punching Bag

Going into the 2012 elections, Obama was receiving regularly high approval ratings on foreign policy and generally looked more in touch with reality than Mitt Romney, who seemed stuck in Cold War preoccupations with Russia and with obsolete measurements of national security. The crisis in Ukraine that exploded in March 2014 and simmered the rest of the year steadily undermined perceptions of Obama's strategic vision and tactical competence, while retroactively (at least in the eyes of conservative opinion leaders) making Romney look like a prophet.

But even without hostile spin, Putin's aggressive behavior (compounded by steadily deteriorating conditions in the Middle East) wrong-footed Obama's famous "strategic tilt" to an Asia-focused foreign policy and made him, not Republicans, seem out of touch with global events.

From Osama's Assassin to Underestimating ISIS

Similarly Obama's apparent mastery of counterterrorism, as evidenced by the killing of Osama bin Laden, seemed to unravel given his unfortunate description of the ISIS-linked organizations as representing a "junior varsity of terrorism." This was followed by an extended period of apparent irresolution about how to confront the new/old threat, even as videos of ISIS fighters beheading Western journalists regularly exploded onto social media sites and then mainstream media.

At the same time, growing public perceptions of ISIS as a major threat indirectly undermined Obama's signature foreign policy accomplishment, the withdrawal of US troops from Iraq and Afghanistan, as critics (including his own former secretary of defense, Leon Panetta)[5] claimed he had ignored advice urging him to keep a "residual" troop presence in Iraq.

From 2012 to 2002 Redux

Even more subtly, the post-GWOT (global war on terrorism) atmosphere that accompanied much of Obama's first term was replaced by something like a return to the public opinion and media environment of 2002, with inchoate fears of terrorist threats to the homeland spiking and even a return to talk of "security moms" (women suddenly receptive to GOP national-security appeals).

Even as Obama's approval ratings on foreign policy and national security eroded, the reported salience of such issues in the constellation of public concerns steadily climbed.[6]

From Comprehensive Immigration Reform to Managing Porous Borders

A final bit of bad luck for Obama and Democrats was a sudden outbreak of two perceived crises that strongly affected already shaky public confidence in border security. The first was an upsurge of southern border crossings by unaccompanied minors, mostly from Central America, that began attracting major media attention in the summer of 2014. Because anti-human-trafficking laws created significant procedural protections for children from non-contiguous countries, there was no way quickly to deport them, and the temporary measures used to house them in areas away from the border reinforced the impression of a "crisis." Without question, this phenomenon—the severity of which quickly abated—spurred a strong boost particularly but not exclusively among Republican voters, in sentiment opposing any "path to citizenship" for the undocumented and actually favoring mass deportations.

Just as the refugee border crisis subsided, an even larger perceived crisis broke out over fears that West Africa's Ebola outbreak would spread to and within the

US because of inadequate border security and a supposedly incompetent public health system.

Lurid fears of immigrants and refugees pouring across an allegedly porous border harboring ISIS terrorists and deadly diseases began seeping into Republican rhetoric and campaign ads. New Hampshire US Senate candidate Scott Brown was most systematic in weaving together these themes, as noted by *The Guardian*'s Jon Swaine:

> [New Hampshire] could not seem further away from the Islamic State's desert plains, the Ebola-stricken villages of west Africa or the badlands beneath the southern US border.
>
> Scott Brown, a Republican who claims to be that Mr Fixit, manages to combine all three emergencies into one nightmarish threat that he says is facing Americans.
>
> "I think it's all connected," said Brown, when asked during a radio interview last month whether the US should place restrictions on travelers from west Africa. "We have a border that's so porous that anyone can walk across it. I think it's naive to think that people aren't going to be walking through here who have those types of diseases and/or other types of intent—criminal or terrorist." [7]

As the president's approval ratings remained stubbornly low and Republicans seemed to be gaining traction in turning his past advantages into disadvantages, it was no surprise that in the red states (those carried by Romney in 2012) Democratic candidates tended to stress their independence from the president—especially incumbents like Begich of Alaska, Pryor of Arkansas, Landrieu of Louisiana, and Hagan of North Carolina, who could boast of their own accomplishments and their occasional high-profile disagreements with Obama (most notably energy issues important to voters in Alaska, Arkansas, and Louisiana).

But there and elsewhere, Democrats did pursue some national themes of their own.

The Minimum Wage Fight

Beginning almost immediately after the 2012 elections, Democrats, having struggled to find an issue that galvanized public concerns over stagnant wages and economic inequality in a way that differentiated them from the GOP, quickly began to coalesce around demands for a higher national (and outside Washington, state and even local) minimum wage. The initial vehicle was a bill sponsored by Tom Harkin in the Senate and George Miller in the House raising the federal minimum wage from $7.25 to $10.10 per hour, with a subsequent indexing to reflect rising costs of living. President Obama endorsed the legislation in his 2014 State of the Union address and then took a proactive step in that direction with an executive order establishing a $10.10 minimum wage for private-sector workers engaged in new federal contracts.[8]

It is safe to say no item of Democratic messaging from that point on until November failed to include a pitch for a higher minimum wage. Most Republicans found ways to reject, ignore, or deflect such proposals (usually citing the impact on unemployment for marginal or entry-level workers or claiming it unfairly benefited children or second earners from well-off families), though a few prominent Republicans, most notably Mitt Romney, dissented and argued Republicans should favor a higher minimum wage.[9]

Democrats derived considerable hope from polls throughout the cycle, showing that a minimum wage increase was widely popular. A Pew survey in January showed that Americans supported the $10.10 minimum wage by nearly a three-to-one margin, with a majority of Republicans and 71 percent of independents concurring.[10]

The War on Women and the GOP Response

A secondary theme popular among Democrats in many states was that Republicans were engaged in a "war on women" via obstruction of equal-pay legislation and hostility to basic reproductive rights. While "war on women" gradually became a designation used by conservatives to mock gender-based Democratic appeals, there's no question that Democrats in many states sought to exploit state-level Republican legislative initiatives restricting abortion rights or shutting down clinics. Democrats also explored the implications of the GOP's 2012 campaign for "religious liberty" that rejected mandated health insurance coverage of contraceptives as objectionable to religious employers. Extremist positions by Republican candidates themselves—particularly endorsement of "personhood" initiatives that might ban certain contraceptives or even in vitro fertility treatments—drew attention from Democrats as well.

Republicans who were the target of such attacks often deflected or ignored them; it became exceptionally common for GOP candidates in this cycle to assert they were not "focused" on cultural issues or that they did not represent a "priority."[11] Some devised clever counter-punching tactics. Louisiana Gov. Bobby Jindal's idea that pro-life politicians should endorse over-the-counter distribution of standard oral contraceptives (not including, of course, Plan B contraception) was avidly picked up by Colorado Senate candidate Cory Gardner, under sustained attack by Mark Udall's campaign for his past endorsement (recently abandoned) of a personhood initiative.[12] North Carolina Senate candidate Thom Tillis also embraced this position.

In general, Republican handling of cultural issues in 2014 reflected the broader GOP/media narrative according to which Republicans had eschewed extremism in favor of "pragmatism" and strictly avoided the kind of extended arguments that had gotten candidates in trouble in the past. A classic example was provided by Iowa's Joni Ernst in a debate with Bruce Braley in which he brought up her sponsorship of a state constitutional amendment that would have established personhood for zygotes from the moment an ovum was fertilized. Here was her response: "The amendment that is being referenced by the congressman would not do any of the things that you stated it would do. . . . That amendment is simply a statement that I support life."[13] That was her story, and she was sticking to it, even though legal experts generally agree that constitutionally conferred citizenship rights are not just a symbolic gesture.

As it turns out, Ernst and other Republican Senate candidates went through a sort of boot-camp training in how not to respond to questions about their exotic cultural views, heavily influenced by the experience of imploding Republican candidacies in 2010 and 2012. The 2014 candidates might have positions on abortion as extreme as, say, 2012's poster boy for self-destruction, Missouri's Todd Akin. But none of them would emulate his drift into speculation about a woman's body protecting her from pregnancy in cases of "legitimate rape."[14]

Sometimes the answer is simply to refuse to talk about it, and that was a common tactic for Republicans in 2014. This both fed and was made possible by "the disciplined GOP is moving to the center" media narrative that half-discredited Democratic attacks before they were even launched.

The dynamics of individual races, however, continued to vary significantly.

Senate

Alaska

Two universally noted features of the Sullivan-Begich race were the historic difficulty of polling in Alaska and the heroic nature of Democratic GOTV efforts in a state with a small population scattered across a vast geographic landscape.

But the race was also the scene of a tactical error by Begich's campaign that backfired immediately: a late-August ad accusing Sullivan of negotiating a lenient plea deal with a sex offender who committed a brutal murder during his tenure as attorney general of Alaska.[15] The ad was pulled after the family of the victims protested, but it was immediately cited as among the worst "dirty politics" maneuvers of the cycle.

In September, election forecaster Nate Silver of *FiveThirtyEight* analyzed Alaska polling in recent elections and concluded they systematically overestimated Democratic performance by a significant extent. (Begich won his Senate seat in 2008 by an eyelash after polls had him leading incumbent Ted Stevens by an average of 8 percent.[16]) But Democratic hopes concentrated on the local Bannock Street Project turnout effort. An October 4 article by the *Washington Post's* Phillip Rucker summed up these hopes not only for Begich but for other embattled Democratic Senate candidates in close races:

> The Democrats' showcase is Alaska, where neither party previously had much grass-roots infrastructure because of its Republican tilt and the logistical obstacles of traveling between rural villages. . . .
>
> Sullivan has five field offices in the state's most-populated areas, just as Begich did during his 2008 campaign. But this year, Begich opened 16 offices, many in far-flung communities.
>
> Whereas Sullivan and the Republican Party have 14 field staffers on the payroll, Begich and the Democratic Party have 90. Nearly half of them are based in rural Alaska and are responsible for on-the-ground organizing in the state's 198 Native villages. . . .
>
> "We have knocked on every single door in rural Alaska," Begich said in an interview. "This is unbelievable. No one's ever done it like this—ever."[17]

So said—or hoped—Democratic activists in nearly every Senate battleground state.

Arkansas

This contest was in some respects the "classic" of the cycle. The Democratic incumbent, Mark Pryor, had the benefit of a famous family name, considerable Senate seniority, a "centrist" reputation, and a history of being politically invulnerable in Arkansas. (He did not even draw a Republican opponent in 2008.) His handpicked Republican challenger, US Rep. Tom Cotton, had an A-list resume (Harvard Law School, combat service in both Iraq and Afghanistan, a job with McKinsey & Co.) and the high regard of virtually every Beltway Republican faction (especially defense hawks), among whom it was not unusual to hear him described as a future president.

Hanging over the contest were signs that Arkansas was finally undergoing the full realignment of rural and small-town white voters to the GOP that had happened earlier in most southern states. In 2010, Pryor's senior colleague, Blanche Lincoln, was routed by nineteen points (albeit after winning a bitter primary over a labor-backed candidate). In 2012, Republicans won control of the state legislature for the first time since Reconstruction.

Thus Cotton had every reason to campaign as a generic Republican, which he largely did, while Pryor spent the campaign hammering away at him for votes against a farm bill and a minimum wage hike.[18] Democrats also took some hope in the fact that the state had an exceptionally unmobilized African American electorate (in part thanks to having never been targeted nationally); according to one measurement, the African American turnout rate in the state was the second lowest in the country in 2012.[19] But the black vote in Arkansas, aside from being relatively small (15 percent of the voting age population as of 2010),[20] was also less urban than in most parts of the country, which made GOTV efforts more expensive and complicated.

For much of the year, Pryor was a model of Senate Democratic durability, having been widely written off before the year ended, but was still running close to or even ahead of Cotton. By late September, however, Cotton was opening up a significant if still narrow (single-digit) lead in most polls.[21]

Colorado

The home of the actual Bannock Street—address of Michael Bennet's 2010 campaign headquarters—held a Senate contest that in some respects felt like a rerun. Like Ken Buck, Cory Gardner was vulnerable on reproductive rights issues. Like Bennet, Mark Udall decided to make that the centerpiece of his campaign, in a highly targeted appeal to white women. The 2012 Obama campaign had also focused its Colorado campaign on Romney's pro-life record and made white women (along with Latinos of both genders) the primary target of its GOTV efforts.

The big question coming down the home stretch in 2014 was whether this messaging strategy had grown stale, especially given Gardner's aggressive prophylactic efforts to rebrand himself as a moderate on reproductive rights issues via a repudiation of Colorado's relentless personhood movement and adoption of Bobby Jindal's clever technique of embracing over-the-counter sales of oral contraceptives. The possibility that Colorado Democrats were overdoing this particular message in Udall's campaign was encapsulated by jibes referring to the incumbent senator as "Mark Uterus."[22]

The other variable in Colorado that made 2014 different from 2010 (but in a way that provided additional encouragement to Democrats) is that the state had formally moved from a system heavily relying on mail ballots to an all-mail-ballot system, a step expected to boost turnout.[23]

Georgia

David Perdue began the general election campaign as a solid favorite over Michelle Nunn. Despite more than a year of fears that the huge Republican Senate field and a very long runoff period would lead to a bloodily bruised and financially depleted nominee, Perdue came out of the runoff leading a united GOP able to count on significant national Republican financial help, with Perdue's own deep pockets as a final resort. He had no public record to criticize, and the conspicuous tilt-to-the-right gestures he made during the primary and runoff—savagely attacking immigration "amnesty," disclaiming support for Common Core education standards, and saying he wouldn't support Mitch McConnell for Senate party leader—were generally regarded either as "dog whistle" appeals to conservative activists or poll-tested positions that were actually popular in Georgia.

Most of all, Perdue had the backstop of a January runoff if he fell just a bit short of 50 percent or even if he trailed Nunn narrowly. On every occasion the state had held general election runoffs for major offices, the Republicans won easily thanks to low and skewed turnout. (Democratic incumbent Wyche Fowler lost a runoff to

Paul Coverdell in 1992, and Republican incumbent Saxby Chambliss won another against Jim Martin in 2008.)

Nunn's big break (or so it seemed at the time) occurred at the beginning of October when *Politico* reported on a nine-year-old deposition in a bankruptcy proceeding for a company Perdue had run:

> During a July 2005 deposition, a transcript of which was provided to *Politico*, Perdue spoke at length about his role in Pillowtex's collapse, which led to the loss of more than 7,600 jobs. Perdue was asked about his "experience with outsourcing," and his response was blunt.
>
> "Yeah, I spent most of my career doing that," Perdue said, according to the 186-page transcript of his sworn testimony.
>
> The Georgia Republican then listed his career experience, much of which involved outsourcing.[24]

Challenged about the comment a few days later, Perdue compounded the gaffe by saying he was "proud" of his involvement in outsourcing and then drifted into murky economic rationalizations along with attacks on big government for making outsourcing necessary to turn a profit.[25] The Nunn campaign (which had previously focused on its own candidate's pledges to revive her father's tradition of bipartisanship in the Senate) quickly pounced, understanding it had found a way (much as the Obama campaign did in 2012) to paint its opponent as a corporate predator who was decidedly *not* "on your side," while also undermining Perdue's sole credential for office—his claims to be a "job creator." For a brief period of time, national political observers from both parties thought Perdue might be in free fall, but an infusion of "outside" money for ads continuing to tie Nunn to Barack Obama appeared to stabilize his campaign going into election day. Both campaigns focused heavily on early voting, and Democrats were cautiously encouraged by indications of a relatively high percentage of African Americans voting early, with a significant number being reported as not having participated in the 2010 elections.[26]

Iowa

In no Senate race did a single moment have such a major impact: the appearance in March of a YouTube video (uploaded, ironically, by a Braley supporter) in which US Rep. Bruce Braley, the unopposed Democratic candidate to succeed Tom Harkin, was shown speaking at a fundraiser being held on his behalf by a group of Texas trial lawyers. Here's the crucial text:

> To put this in stark contrast, if you help me win this race, you may have someone with your background, your experience, your voice, someone's who's been literally fighting tort reform for 30 years in a visible and public way on the Senate Judiciary Committee or you might have a farmer from Iowa who never went to law school, never practiced law, serving as the next chair of the Senate Judiciary Committee. Because if Democrats lose the majority, Chuck Grassley will be the next chair of the Senate Judiciary Committee.[27]

Braley committed multiple gaffes here. Iowans as a whole are pretty seriously invested in the seniority of their senators. Considering the ideological chasm separating Tom Harkin and Chuck Grassley, there are a surprising number of Iowans in the habit of voting for both of them. Disrespecting Grassley, disrespecting his shot at a major Senate committee chairmanship, and most of all disrespecting Iowa farmers all rapidly erased the advantage many observers thought Braley held as Harkin's chosen successor, particularly in view of his "head start" over a fairly undistinguished Republican field. (The state's two Republican US House members, Steve King and Tom Latham, both passed up the race.) And while it took a while for this to become apparent, the Braley video turned out to play into the campaign theme of one particular Republican challenger, Joni Ernst, whose folksy, farm-flavored "Make 'em squeal" ad[28] that launched her toward a big primary victory might have been designed as an answer to the cynical-trial-lawyer persona created by Braley's deadly pander to the trial lawyers.

With the race virtually even after the primary, Ernst continued with iterations of her "biography"—a mother, soldier (a high-ranking member of the National Guard, deployed in both wars in Iraq), and farm-bred "Iowa nice" itching to bring common sense and pork-busting prudence to Washington. Braley and his allies counterattacked with ads mining Ernst's rich history of hyperconservative comments and issue positions—notably a hostility to minimum wage laws and a willingness to consider major changes to Social Security and Medicare. (Braley would later focus on Ernst's extremist cultural positions, a tactic that she was well-prepared to parry, as noted above.)

But even as Braley tried to get the contest onto a more favorable, issue-oriented landscape, he was hit with

another "character issue" that nicely meshed with the
traitor-to-Iowa, trial-lawyer persona he seemed to exhibit
in the Texas fundraiser appearance. Around the beginning of August, word leaked out from the homeowners'
association in a lakeside development where Braley
and his wife owned a vacation property that they had
hinted at possible legal action against a neighbor whose
pet free-range chickens were defecating on the Braleys'
lawn. Almost immediately, America Rising, the national
Republican-affiliated group responsible for opposition
research, showed up in the area to interview the neighbor for a Super PAC attack ad, and the "chicken lawsuit"
became a staple of the campaign, along with the "Disrespecting Iowa Farmer Chuck Grassley" meme. Ernst herself became adept at tying it all together: "You threaten
to sue somebody because a chicken's on your property?
That's absolutely ridiculous. In Red Oak, my neighbor
next door, when we first moved into our house, their
kids were raising chickens in the garage as a project.
No big deal. Oh, my goodness. It's Iowa. Come on. Get
over yourself."[29]

This is the sort of "debate" that led *Slate*'s David Weigel
in mid-August to call the Iowa contest "America's dumbest Senate race."[30]

Kentucky

Mitch McConnell's reelection campaign was a natural
media focus even after he crushed Tea Party candidate
Matt Bevin in a May primary. After celebrity Democrat
Ashley Judd lengthily considered and finally decided
against a challenge to McConnell—though not after an

account leaked of McConnell and his political advisors coolly discussing how they would tear Judd apart with ads questioning her mental health and religious views[31]— Democrats successfully recruited Alison Lundergan Grimes, Kentucky secretary of state and daughter of a former state party chair.

As a long-standing national party leader in one of the most despised Congresses ever, McConnell had low approval numbers in Kentucky (as well as everywhere else). But McConnell also had access to virtually unlimited funds and ran perhaps the most obsessively anti-Obama campaign in the country, taking special advantage of the strong antipathy toward the administration in "coal country," including traditionally Democratic areas, thanks to the Environmental Protection Agency's proposed and pending regulations restricting carbon emissions by utilities—a.k.a. "Obama's war on coal."

Still, despite widespread predictions of a McConnell win, Grimes hung in and even pulled ahead in one early October poll.[32] As a sign of varying opinions about the trajectory of the race, the DSCC pulled ads on Grimes' behalf in mid-October,[33] only to reenter the state with money in hand a week later.[34]

Mid-October also witnessed a moment (or two) that exemplified the red-state Democratic plight, as reported by NBC's Perry Bacon Jr.:

Grimes' refusal to answer if she voted for President Barack Obama in 2012 during a taped session with *The Courier-Journal* on Thursday turned into a viral video seen across the country—with Republicans, the press and even some Democrats ripping her for the non-response. But in a debate with U.S. Senator and Republican Leader Mitch McConnell Monday here, the Kentucky secretary of state again declined to say if she backed the president of her own party, trying to avoid any association with Obama, who is deeply unpopular in Kentucky.[35]

Grimes's determination not to admit she voted for Obama became grist for debates among political strategists about its wisdom or folly. It also served as an occasion for many a midelection and postelection complaint from Democrats about the "cowardice" of their party brethren in "enemy territory," which some blamed for a lack of rank-and-file "enthusiasm" in the party.[36]

Louisiana

Louisiana's Senate race was from the beginning sui generis because of the state's "jungle primary" system, in which candidates without respect to party compete in a single event coinciding with the general election nationally and then (if no one wins a majority) the top two finishers participate in a December runoff. There was a brief lapse in the use of the jungle primary federal offices in 2008, when Democrat Mary Landrieu won a general election majority over Republican John Kennedy. But she won a jungle primary runoff in December 2002—a rare Democratic accomplishment.

Landrieu's reputation as a successful electoral scrapper dated back to her first election in 1996, in a disputed nail biter over Republican Woody Jenkins that left the seat in limbo for months until a Republican-controlled

Senate finally gave up on "voter fraud" investigations and seated her. (A favorite humorous New Orleans t-shirt in the aftermath bore the legend "I voted for Mary Landrieu three times and all I got was this lousy t-shirt!")

But aside from the return of the jungle primary for federal races, which made assembling a November 4 majority very difficult, Landrieu faced several negative trends in this cycle: a sizable drop in the state's African American population after Hurricane Katrina; an ongoing realignment of white Catholic voters—once the mainstay of her family's political appeal—toward the GOP; and the deteriorating Louisiana popularity of the president, aggravated by collisions over energy and environmental issues such as the Keystone XL pipeline.[37]

Perhaps the most surprising development in the general election campaign was an actual lawsuit alleging that Landrieu was ineligible for the ballot because she no longer had a residence in Louisiana.[38] It's hard to think of a senator with deeper roots in a home state; Landrieu's father and brother have both served as mayors of New Orleans. She argued that she lived in the house jointly owned by her mother and herself and eight siblings when in the state, and the suit was dismissed.

Landrieu's major opponent was US Rep. Bill Cassidy, but due to multiple minor candidates (including one Tea Party favorite, Rob Maness), it became very clear the race would go to a runoff unless Landrieu experienced a late surge of support. Shortly before Election Day, pollsters began focusing on a Landrieu-Cassidy runoff, showing Landrieu in serious trouble as Democratic and Democratic-leaning voters appeared less likely than Republicans to show up a second time.[39]

New Hampshire

Republicans were pleased and Democrats were somewhat less than threatened when (briefly) former Massachusetts US Senator Scott Brown announced a bid to unseat Sen. Jeanne Shaheen of New Hampshire. Yes, Brown had run a skillful January 2010 special election campaign against the hapless Martha Coakley. But he subsequently lost in 2012 to Elizabeth Warren and would face the "carpetbagger" charge for having switched states (though not so much in media markets, since Boston media blanket much of the Granite State).

Shaheen held a modest to robust lead in the polls for months,[40] and the race nearly fell from the list of battleground contests. But down the stretch, often to the bafflement of political observers, Brown began to close in on the incumbent. The only factor that made much sense in explaining the race (other than the likely voter patterns that made even Massachusetts competitive) was Brown's unusually heavy emphasis on national security themes (as pointed out above). Since Shaheen's personal favorability ratings remained positive throughout the race, the New Hampshire contest is one sure to be cited by those looking for evidence that Republicans succeeded in "nationalizing" the midterms.

North Carolina

Unlike most battleground-state Republican candidates, Thom Tillis appeared to be running consistently just behind Kay Hagan for most of the general election campaign. Of all the efforts around the country to "localize" a congressional race, Hagan's may have been the most successful, insofar as she exploited Tillis's leadership position in an unpopular Republican controlled state legislature. To an extent exceeded perhaps only by Sam Brownback's Kansas, North Carolina had been conducting an ideological experiment under the whip of Art Pope, a wealthy libertarian-ish ally of the Koch brothers who heavily contributed to GOP state legislative candidates, funded a conservative state think tank that churned out legislative ideas, and then set about implementing them as Gov. Pat McCrory's budget director.[41] While Pope and company promoted a broad conservative agenda heavy with voting restrictions and cultural gestures, their most controversial actions involved reduced education spending in a state with a long history of pride in public education. Tillis seemed to be paying a price for his state party's hubris throughout most of the campaign.

His own campaign mostly relied on cookie-cutter attacks on Hagan for complicity in Obamacare and general responsibility for the president's record, though it also unearthed Hagan's criticism of Elizabeth Dole in 2008 for having sponsored no significant legislation and turned it on her.

In September and early October, sudden Republican crises in two contests—one in Kansas, one in South Dakota—previously considered to be safe for the GOP temporarily upset previous calculations.

Kansas

A "centrist" independent candidacy by entrepreneur Greg Orman did not at first seem to be a particular threat to Pat Roberts, even damaged as he was by an unimpressive primary win. But then on September 3, Democratic candidate Chad Taylor withdrew and endorsed Orman, who almost immediately vaulted into a sizable lead that set off alarm bells throughout the national GOP.[42]

Orman took a mix of positions associated with Democrats (modest gun control, infrastructure investment) and Republicans (entitlement reform), but he mainly campaigned on a determination to force bipartisan cooperation, in part by a pledge to caucus (if control was in question) with the party most willing to compromise with his agenda. Republicans immediately accused him in this heavily Republican state of being a stealth Democrat preparing to save Harry Reid's majority. Just as important, Senate Republicans forced Roberts to let them take over his campaign, sending crack national staff in for a rescue mission, with plenty of fresh funds. After trailing by double digits as late as September, Roberts had largely closed the gap by Election Day.

South Dakota

This state made a brief but dramatic appearance on the Senate battleground the first week of October when at least one poll[43] (in a contest without a lot of polling) showed independent candidate and former Republican Senator Larry Pressler within a few points of Gov. Mike Rounds, who had suffered chronic, nagging bad publicity over the state's questionable operation of an unpopular federal program that gave foreign investors access to US citizenship.[44] Like Kansas' Orman, Pressler indicated he would decide in January which party he would caucus with, which created the specter of Senate control being decided by one or two eccentrics long after election day—a picture also complicated by a probable December runoff in Louisiana and a possible January runoff in Georgia. Democrats, who had written off their own South Dakota candidate, Rick Weiland, much earlier, came back into the state with ads designed to win a close three-way race.[45] Then new polls came out, showing Rounds back up handily with Pressler running a poor third, and the excitement over South Dakota subsided as quickly as it erupted.

There were three other contests considered potentially competitive early in the cycle that had slipped off the board by the stretch run.

Michigan

Republican Terri Lynn Land appeared to be in a close race with US Rep. Gary Peters for the seat of retiring Sen. Carl Levin until late summer, when she slipped in the polls and donors began to pull out. Thomas Beaumont of the Associated Press chronicled the quick devolution of Land's campaign:

> Americans for Prosperity, the flagship group of billionaire conservative brothers Charles and David Koch, stopped advertising for Land this summer, after spending $5.1 million in ads supporting her through June, but describing the race as "an uphill climb."

Likewise, the U.S. Chamber of Commerce, which endorsed Land, ran $400,000 in ads, but has not since June.

The most recent red flag for Land came last month when Freedom Partners, a group associated with the Kochs, canceled an $878,000 ad purchase that was to run in Michigan throughout August.

"There is a high interest in return on investment," James Davis of Freedom Partners said. "We make decisions based on the most effective use for each dollar at that time."[46]

Land was left wondering exactly how much of her personal fortune she'd need to spend to keep up the facade of impending victory.

Land, who has already contributed more than $3 million of her own, declined to say if she'll be forced to spend more of her own money to keep up.

"You need to invest what you're capable of," Land said in an Associated Press interview in Marshall. "We're going to work hard and do that."

Hesitant to say so publicly, some Michigan and national GOP officials say Land was not their first choice. They tried recruiting U.S. Reps. Mike Rogers or Dave Camp, after Land put her name forward last year.[47]

Oregon

Republicans were pleased to recruit pediatric surgeon Monica Wehby—a "culturally liberal, fiscally conservative" candidate who had gotten some publicity as an early critic of the Affordable Care Act—to run against freshman Sen. Jeff Merkley, figuring she'd be well-equipped to take advantage of the botched rollouts of both the national and the Oregon Obamacare enrollment websites.

Shortly before Oregon's May 20 primary, though, Wehby was hit with two anonymously sourced but apparently accurate accounts of erratic domestic behavior, one involving alleged stalking of an ex-boyfriend[48] and another extending to physical violence against a soon-to-be-ex-husband.[49] The allegations came out too late to keep Wehby from winning her primary (in Oregon's all-mail-ballot electoral system, most voters had already cast ballots by the time they heard of the allegations) but not too early to cripple the beginning of her general election campaign.

Wehby's struggling effort was later afflicted with not one but two embarrassing incidents where her campaign website's health care section was found to have lifted language word-for-word from unattributed sources. (Karl Rove's fundraising outfit, American Crossroads, was one of the sources;[50] one of Wehby's primary opponents was another.[51]) The first allegation, by *BuzzFeed*, led to one of the more hilariously brazen damage-control efforts of the cycle: "'The suggestion that a pediatric neurosurgeon needs to copy a health care plan from American Crossroads is absurd,' a Wehby campaign spokesman told BuzzFeed News. 'Dr. Wehby is too busy performing brain surgery on sick children to respond, sorry.'"[52]

Wehby never recovered.

Virginia

A final potentially close race that Republicans dreamed about was Virginia, where highly regarded former RNC chairman Ed Gillespie surprisingly took on Mark Warner. Every single poll[53] of the race showed Warner up by double digits until a final survey from Christopher Newport University had Gillespie within seven points. A few tsunami-mad Republican spinners chortled at the thought of an upset in Virginia, but most Democrats weren't worried—until election night, when Warner won far more narrowly than anyone seriously expected.

House

As the general election campaign got fully under way in the summer, Democrats had a slight lead in the generic congressional ballot, though not one large enough to survive the anticipated early autumn "switchover" in polls from registered voters to likely voters, which typically produces an improvement in Republican numbers, especially in midterms. The exceptionally low number of competitive House races (well under fifty in most assessments throughout the year) made huge GOP gains like those of 2010 extremely unlikely.

In early January, the authoritative Cook Political Report identified forty-five competitive (as defined by districts that were either toss-ups or leaned toward one party or the other) House districts, twenty-four of them occupied by Democrats and twenty-one by Republicans. A rash of Republican retirements created eight "open" and competitive Republican-held seats as opposed to just one open competitive Democratic-held seat. But the projections showed ten Democrats in the more vulnerable toss-up category as opposed to just four Republicans.[54]

Still, the landscape was vastly better for Democrats than at the beginning of 2010, when they held thirty-nine of fifty competitive seats.[55] And while the number of competitive seats ultimately swelled from fifty to eighty-seven in 2010, it modestly shrank in 2014 from forty-four to thirty-nine.

An early bellwether was a special election in Florida's thirteenth district in March for a Tampa Bay–area seat vacated by the death of veteran Republican Bill Young. The district had been trending Democratic and was narrowly carried by Barack Obama in 2012. Democrats recruited a star candidate in Alex Sink, who ran a competitive race against Rick Scott for governor in 2010 and was facing David Jolly, a former Young staffer turned lobbyist—not the best resume line for 2014. After a $13 million contest, with roughly $9 million spent by outside groups[56] (the bulk of it aimed at helping Jolly overcome Sink's fund-raising advantage, mostly by attacking Obamacare), Jolly pulled a mild but significant upset.[57]

Gubernatorial Contests

There were an unusually large number of close gubernatorial races going into the heat of the general election, with incumbents and incumbent successors of both parties looking to be in some trouble, as one might expect given the heavily "wrong-track" sentiments of the voting public.

Vulnerable Democrats included Pat Quinn of Illinois, Dan Malloy of Connecticut, Neil Abercrombie of Hawaii, Martha Coakley (succeeding Deval Patrick) of Massachusetts, and Mike Ross (succeeding Mike Beebe) of Arkansas. Later in the cycle, Maggie Hassan of New Hampshire, John Hickenlooper of Colorado, Anthony Brown of Maryland (succeeding Martin O'Malley), and late primary winner Gina Raimondo of Rhode Island (succeeding Lincoln Chafee) emerged as vulnerable.

Abercrombie lost decisively in an August primary, but initially Democrats feared winner David Ige could lose to Duke Aiona thanks to the independent candidacy of Mufi Hanneman.

Vulnerable Republicans included Paul LePage of Maine (benefiting again from an independent candidacy by Eliot Cutler), Tom Corbett of Pennsylvania, Rick Scott of Florida, Rick Snyder of Michigan, Nathan Deal of Georgia, and Sam Brownback of Kansas. Late in the cycle, Sean Parnell of Alaska emerged as a very vulnerable incumbent when the Democratic gubernatorial candidate withdrew and became the running mate of independent Bill Walker, who disagreed strongly with Parnell over petroleum taxes (and was eventually endorsed by Sarah Palin, whose resignation made Parnell governor).

Florida

From beginning to end, the 2014 Florida governor's race was a tough, expensive contest between the state's last two governors, incumbent Rick Scott and predecessor (and Republican-turned-Democrat) Charlie Crist. Scott entered 2014 with serious popularity issues,[58] and in the course of the campaign, never succeeded in achieving a positive approval-rating ratio. His strategy, however, focused on constant efforts to contrast Florida's economic conditions during his term to those in Crist's (who was, of course, governor during the national economic crisis of 2008–9). Scott also enjoyed roughly a two-to-one advantage in campaign spending on ads during 2014 (which totaled roughly $100 million).[59]

One hopeful sign for the Crist camp down the stretch was that Democrats seemed to be cutting into the traditional GOP advantage in early voting (heavily tilted toward by-mail absentee ballots). An incident in a final debate between the two, in which Scott appeared to act petulantly about Crist's use of a fan beneath his podium, got a lot of media attention, feeding Democratic hopes that undecideds would break to Crist.

Georgia

Like his predecessor, two-term Gov. Sonny Perdue (cousin of 2014 GOP Senate candidate David Perdue), Nathan Deal was a longtime conservative Democrat (a member of the US House from 1993 to 2011) who switched parties as the state began its ideological realignment toward the Republican Party. He won his first term in 2010 after a bitter primary, runoff, and general election, defeating former Secretary of State (and 2014 Senate candidate) Karen Handel for the GOP nomination and then disposing of Georgia's last Democratic governor, Roy Barnes.

Deal entered the 2014 cycle in reasonably good shape, despite being dogged by an old corruption allegation and an alleged cover-up, a controversial publicly financed stadium deal, and sustained ambivalence over the Common Core education standards, for which Perdue had been a national leader. The contest was transformed when Democratic state senator Jason Carter, grandson of the thirty-ninth president, entered the race, and like his ticket mate (and fellow political scion) Michelle Nunn became instantly competitive in both fundraising and the polls. As the race occasionally tightened, a shadow was frequently cast by Georgia's atavistic majority-vote requirement for general election victories, with runoffs set at different dates for state (December 2) and federal (January 6) offices. With an active Libertarian candidate (Andrew Hunt) in the governor's race attracting as much as 7 percent in the polls,[60] a runoff seemed entirely possible.

Carter benefited from running in a state with a key Senate race, bringing with it the GOTV investment and technology of the Bannock Street Project. Democratic early voting efforts in Georgia appeared effective in attracting new voters and in boosting the minority percentage of early voters. (Georgia has no party registration, but the state does release information on racial voting patterns.)

Illinois

Going into 2014, Pat Quinn, who took office when Rod Blagojevich was impeached and removed from office for corruption in 2009, was regularly cited as one of the least popular governors in America. In May 2013, Micah Cohen of the *New York Times* compiled average approval ratings for all the governors dating back to the beginning of 2012,[61] and Quinn, with 33 percent positive and 52 percent negative ratings, was second to last (behind only Lincoln Chafee of Rhode Island, who subsequently decided against running for another term). Quinn was struggling with multiple issues beyond lagging midterm turnout for Democrats. General "wrong-track" sentiment about the Illinois government was widespread, which was not surprising since Quinn's two immediate predecessors did prison time for corruption. He alienated many public employees with legislation overhauling the state's terribly underfunded pension system;[62] he then championed a temporary income tax increase for individuals and businesses to close a chronic budget shortfall and subsequently proposed making it permanent.[63]

The environment in Illinois was ideal for an "outsider business executive" candidate like Bruce Rauner, who self-funded his primary win over three state-government veterans. However, Rauner's wealth and how he earned it (as a private equity manager) made him the target of attack ads reminiscent of those the Obama campaign ran against Mitt Romney in 2012. And speaking of Obama, Illinois is one of the few states where the president's approval rating remained at or above 50 percent during the cycle; the president actually campaigned for Quinn, whose stretch-run effort depended on boosting African American turnout in and around Chicago.

The race remained close throughout, but both polls and insider analysis suggested Quinn had become a very narrow favorite in the weeks just before November 4.

Kansas

In a counterpoint to what seemed destined to be a strong national Republican year, one of the country's most

Republican states, Kansas, was the site of a major backlash,[64] led to a considerable extent by nominal Republicans against the conservative policy "experiment" of
Gov. (and former US Senator) Sam Brownback. The
incumbent's tax-cut package, explicitly based on supply-
side economic assumptions (with Arthur Laffer himself
brought in to bless it),[65] created both serious cuts in education spending and an ever-worsening fiscal crisis that
threatened the state's credit rating. Even more danger-
ously for Brownback's political security, in 2012 he led
a high-profile "purge" of "moderate Republican" state
senators who opposed his tax plans—a renewal of an old
intraparty fight in Kansas.

So Brownback began the cycle with seriously under-
water approval ratings[66] and facing a burgeoning
"Republicans for Davis" organization supporting his cred-
itable Democratic opponent, State Representative (and
House Democratic Leader) Paul Davis, who began regularly leading polling averages by midsummer.[67] Like other
endangered Republican incumbents, Brownback began
receiving significant financial assistance from the Republican Governors Association. He also got a break in September when it was revealed that in 1998 Davis had been
caught receiving a lap dance in a strip club that was being
raided. (He was an attorney for the club and was then
single.[68]) Brownback benefited indirectly from the "rescue mission" sent to Kansas by national Republicans on
behalf of endangered Senator Pat Roberts, which focused
on mobilizing conservative voters.

Maine

In sharp contrast to Massachusetts GOP gubernatorial candidate Charlie Baker—and for that matter, Maine's own Republican Sen. Susan Collins and former Sen. Olympia Snowe—nobody has ever referred to Paul LePage as a moderate Republican. LePage is an outspoken Tea Party champion widely regarded as a fluke when elected governor in 2010 with only 38 percent of the vote in a very Republican-friendly year (after winning the GOP nomination over a large field with that same 38 percent of the vote), narrowly edging independent candidate Eliot Cutler. LePage never tried to "move to the center" to improve his odds of reelection, spending a good portion of his term battling with Democratic legislators (he set a record for vetoing bills), baiting liberal constituencies (notably African Americans and labor), and generally behaving like a one-term governor. Perhaps his most significant step was in blocking legislation to expand Medicaid under the provisions of the Affordable Care Act, a law he frequently and bitterly attacked.[70]

Maine Democrats spent a good deal of time trying to convince Cutler not to run again in 2014 and then sought to marginalize his campaign. One of Maine's two US House members, Mike Michaud, won the Democratic primary, and it became obvious Cutler would not come close to matching his 2010 numbers. Under intense pressure to drop out late in the campaign, Cutler would not comply; he was benefiting from tactical advertising by the Republican Governors Association. Less than a week before Election Day, Cutler's most prominent supporter, US Senator Angus King (an independent caucusing with Democrats), switched his support to Michaud. Another

complicating factor was a ballot initiative designed to pro-
tect bears that was widely perceived in rural areas as anti-
hunting, which gave otherwise turned-off voters a reason
to go to the polls.

Massachusetts

Attorney General Martha Coakley entered the 2014 contest to succeed retiring two-term Democratic Governor
Deval Patrick with a cloud over her head: her shocking
loss to Scott Brown in the January 2010 special election
to complete the late Ted Kennedy's Senate term. The
Brown victory, which came after a campaign in which
Coakley by general assent made a lot of unforced errors,
cost Democrats their filibuster-proof supermajority in the
Senate and had an important effect on final passage of
the Affordable Care Act (which could still prove to be
very damaging thanks to current litigation over the fine
print of the law).

Coakley went on to earn reelection in November
2010 and rehabilitated her political reputation enough to
become the front-runner in the primary to succeed Patrick. She lost the state Democratic convention endorsement in June to state treasurer and longtime party fixture
Steve Grossman and won a much narrower than expected
primary victory in September over Grossman and liberal
activist favorite Don Berwick. Thus she did not enter the
short general election campaign against Charlie Baker—
the 2010 GOP nominee—with much momentum.

Baker, meanwhile, represented a tradition that was
still living in Massachusetts even as it became virtually
extinct almost everywhere else in the country: moderate

Republicanism. Moderate Republicans, in fact, had governed the state for sixteen years before Patrick's election in 2006. (Baker himself first held public office in the cabinet of Gov. William Weld.) Baker was pro-choice and favored same-sex marriage, and while he opposed Obamacare, he had no problems with the similar state health insurance program that Mitt Romney had inaugurated. He entered the general election campaign in better financial condition than Coakley and immediately began running close to her in the polls. A big moment occurred when the influential liberal newspaper the *Boston Globe* endorsed Baker,[69] essentially calling him a more managerially oriented change of pace from Patrick. But the race remained very close down the stretch.

Pennsylvania

If Pat Quinn, Rick Scott, and Sam Brownback often competed for the "most unpopular governor" designation, Tom Corbett ranked with Maine's Paul LePage among incumbents deemed most likely to lose, thanks to pallid approval ratings and a general lack of enthusiasm for him among Republicans (who nonetheless did not produce a viable primary challenger to him). Elected initially in 2010 in no small part due to voter fatigue with term-limited Democratic incumbent Ed Rendell, Corbett never established himself as anything other than a gaffe-prone caretaker.

The Democratic gubernatorial primary was taken by storm—and by surprise—by wealthy self-funding business executive and former Secretary of Revenue Tom Wolf, who won more than a majority of the primary vote against three well-regarded opponents (US Rep. Allyson Schwatz, State Treasurer Rob McCord, and former federal and state environmental official Katie McGinty). Wolf began the general election contest with a huge lead over the incumbent, and Corbett went into the late stages of the campaign with very poor prospects for reelection.

Wisconsin

Gov. Scott Walker went into this cycle with a well-earned reputation as a polarizing but successful conservative politician, having survived a recall election in 2012 after he became a national labor movement villain for pushing through a closely divided legislature a bill curtailing public employees' collective bargaining rights.

Walker won the recall battle (according to most close observers)[71] in part because Democrats had a divisive and expensive campaign between labor-backed Kathleen Falk and Milwaukee Mayor Tom Barrett (the eventual winner) to choose a theoretical replacement for Walker. The incumbent was able to exploit a loophole in state campaign finance laws as they applied to recall elections to build an enormous war chest, and the few undecided voters were swayed by discomfort about the recall process and figured Walker deserved a full term.

With very few Wisconsin voters not having already made up their minds about Walker, he was favored going into a lower-turnout midterm election. But Democrats managed to recruit a successful business owner, Mary Burke, who did not face significant primary opposition. The race tightened almost immediately and remained very close throughout the summer and early autumn. Burke's main theme was Walker's failure to reach the job-creation goals he set for himself in 2010, while Walker (and more important his independent allies) hit Burke with a variety of personal attacks, including claims her web page had economic development ideas recycled from other states. In the not-too-distant background of the race was the strong possibility of a 2016 presidential run by Walker if he won.

After many seesaw polls, mostly within the margin of error, an October survey by the usually reliable Marquette Law School poll showed Walker suddenly leading outside the margin of error because of a sudden shift in the profile of likely voters, with Republicans showing signs of an enthusiasm gap that mattered.

Preelection Forecasts

On the brink of Election Day, most reputable forecasters were predicting Republican gains in the House of a modest seven to nine seats.[72] *RealClearPolitics*' final polling average for the generic congressional ballot (i.e., the national House popular vote) gave Republicans a 2.4 percent margin.[73]

In the final week, forecasters were nearly all raising estimates of the probability that Republicans would gain control of the Senate into more confident territory: *FiveThirtyEight* to 76 percent, the *New York Times*' Upshot to 70 percent, the *Washington Post*'s Election Lab to 98 percent, the Princeton Election Consortium to 65 percent, *HuffPost Pollster* to 79 percent, and *Daily Kos* to 90 percent.

While fewer prognosticators were looking at gubernatorial races, the University of Virginia-based *Larry Sabato's
Crystal Ball* reflected a solid consensus view that Republicans would lose a net total of three governorships, with
Democrats picking up net two and independents one.[74]

Uncertainty revolved around the relatively large number of close races at every level, the possibility of systemic
polling error (of the sort that significantly overestimated
Democratic performance in 1994 and 2002 and Republican performance in 1998 and 2012), and hopes among
Democrats that shrewd investments in voter targeting
and GOTV might produce votes that weren't picked up by
polls or analysts.[75]

In terms of the marquee Senate-control contest,
despite growing GOP optimism, there was still a decent
possibility that an independent victory in Kansas, a very
slow count in Alaska, and runoffs in Louisiana and Georgia could spoil Republican victory parties on November 4,
even if the reprieve for Harry Reid turned out to be temporary. It was duly noted that mail ballots postmarked
by (or just before) Election Day could still be counted
in Alaska, Iowa, and North Carolina; a very close race in
any of those states might remain unresolved for a week
or more. And though most of the controversy over "voter
fraud" (as alleged by Republicans) or "voter suppression"
(as alleged by Democrats) had focused on early voting
in this particular cycle, there remained the possibility of
legal battles over ballots. Just fourteen years after the presidential election of 2000, anything still seemed possible.

Chapter 4

The Results

Election Day is still central to the imaginations of political junkies everywhere, although pedants will invariably point out that the "day" is increasingly an illusion. Michael McDonald of the University of Florida estimated on November 2 that seventeen million ballots had already been cast and projected that a record-high 27.5 percent of total ballots would be cast before Election Day, with an even higher average in the highly competitive Senate battleground states where the national parties sought to bank an advantage via mobilization of early voting where possible.[1]

As is generally the case, Election Day was a mélange of frantic below-the-surface activity. Those not privileged with behind-the-scenes intel were limited to sporadic and sometimes misleading reports and rumors of turnout patterns and (after 5:30 p.m. EST, when the first "wave" of exit polls were sent to subscribing media networks) much-stepped-on rumors about the "early exits."

Once polls began to close, however, the clouds of uncertainty slowly but steadily dissipated. Election Night on November 4 was for the most part a rising chorus of Republican celebrations.[2] Leaks of early exit polls gave some hope to Democrats in the close Senate races, but they also showed an electorate that resembled that of 2010 in its demographics and its hostility to the president's leadership and the status quo generally. Any fantasies of a big Democratic upset wave were dispelled with the instant 7:00 p.m. EST "call" of Kentucky for Mitch McConnell, who was rolling up huge margins in the coal-producing regions of his state. Equally disturbing to Democrats was the "too close to call" network judgment at about the same time for the Virginia Senate race, which was expected to be a comfortable win for incumbent Mark Warner. New Hampshire was looking close, too, as were (more predictably) Senate races in Georgia (where early returns indicated a likely runoff) and North Carolina and the big gubernatorial race in Florida.

By the time polls closed in sixteen states (and portions of three others) at 8:00 p.m. EST, the big narrative of the night was how many close races were developing. Two hours and change later, the dam began breaking decisively, with Tom Cotton routing Mark Pryor in Arkansas, the "purple state" Senate races in Colorado and Iowa tilting Republican, Rick Scott winning reelection in Florida, Scott Walker winning reelection in Wisconsin, and a shocking GOP gubernatorial win in Maryland appearing from nowhere. Meanwhile the GOP was winning old sieges against House Democratic fortresses in West Virginia (Nick Rahall) and Georgia (John Barrow), and a turnout apocalypse was beginning to appear in New York, where Democrats were losing multiple close House races and also falling far short in their crusade to retake the state senate.

The exact moment when Republican control of the US Senate became guaranteed varied by who was making "calls," but projections that David Perdue had won in Georgia without a runoff, soon followed by a call for Kansas Sen. Pat Roberts and then for Thom Tillis in North Carolina, made the outcome certain. Late returns produced some redemption for Democrats: Sen. Jeanne Shaheen hung on, as did Connecticut Gov. Dan Malloy and Rhode Island Democratic gubernatorial candidate Gina Raimondo, and the entire Republican wave broke before reaching the Pacific Coast. But Republicans' wins in close races continued with gubernatorial victories in Maine (incumbent Paul LePage winning a startling 48 percent of the vote) and Illinois (incumbent Democrat Pat Quinn's improbable resurrection from many months as the least popular governor falling short after all). Happy GOP spinners switched from "wave" to "tsunami" as the preferred nautical metaphor of the evening, and multiple claims for various mandates fought for airspace.

In the end, Republicans gained nine net Senate seats after victories by Alaska candidate Dan Sullivan, delayed by late-arriving mail ballots and slow rural returns, and Louisiana candidate Bill Cassidy, in Louisiana's December 3 runoff. They won no real upsets but instead swept every race deemed as highly competitive other than New Hampshire's (while making Virginia unexpectedly competitive).

GOP House gains reached the upper range of expectations, with twelve net pickups. Republicans defeated eleven incumbent House Democrats. John Barrow of Georgia and Nick Rahall of West Virginia represented red districts that were considered low-hanging—albeit fiercely defended—fruit by Republicans. Another, Carol Shea-Porter of New Hampshire, represented a classic swing district, which she won in 2006, 2008, and 2012 but lost in 2010 and 2014 to the same opponent, Frank Guinta. Four defeated incumbents (Brad Schneider and Bill Enyart of Illinois, Steven Horsford of Nevada, and Pete Gallego of Texas) were freshmen elected narrowly in 2012. Two (Tim Bishop and Dan Maffei) were New Yorkers from swing districts who succumbed to that state's unusually low Democratic turnout. (Maffei actually lost his seat in similar circumstances in 2010 before regaining it in 2012.)

Republicans also picked up five open Democratic seats. Two (Mike McIntyre's North Carolina seventh district and Jim Matheson's Utah fourth district) were seriously red districts that fell easily once entrenched Democratic incumbents retired. Two others (Bruce Braley's Iowa first district and Mike Michaud's Maine second district) were vacated by unsuccessful statewide candidates.

Democrats took out two Republican incumbents who managed to make themselves vulnerable in very friendly districts. One was Lee Terry of Nebraska, who could not overcome a bad public reaction to remarks that he would "dang straight" keep accepting congressional pay during the 2013 government shutdown.[3] The other was Steve Southerland of Florida, an informal liaison between the House GOP leadership and hard-core conservatives, who ran a clumsy campaign against the wrong Democrat, Gwen Graham, whose father, former Governor and Senator Bob Graham, was a regular presence on the campaign trail.[4]

The one open Republican House seat Democrats won was in California, where retiring Rep. Garry Miller's district fell to Democrat Pete Aguilar. In general, the Golden State served as a late firewall for House Democrats, who ultimately won three very close House races initially led by Republicans, in addition to Miller's seat.

Republicans had a net gain of two governorships after being widely expected to suffer losses. (No wave was large enough to lift Pennsylvania's Tom Corbett from defeat, and Alaska's Sean Parnell lost to a strange independent/Democratic "fusion" ticket endorsed by Sarah Palin.) More impressively, they won eleven state legislative chambers, boosting their majority to sixty-eight of ninety-eight (one tied and another nonpartisan). Even in California, where otherwise Republicans lost one net US House seat and every statewide contest, the GOP broke Democratic "supermajorities" in both chambers of the legislature.

The "beating expectations" factor for Republicans could represent a last-minute trend (the conventional meaning of "wave"), or it may simply have been the result of a systemic polling error. Depending on which analysis of which polls you use and during which period late in the campaign, on Election Day, they underestimated Republican performance by an average of somewhere between four and five points in Senate races and a bit less in gubernatorial races. Nate Silver calculates a four-point error in Senate races and argues that it is identical to the polling error in favor of Democrats in 2002 (another and more surprising wave election) and just a bit more than a pro-Republican bias in 2012.[5]

Arguably, though, the GOP victory slightly overperformed (if at all) what you'd expect from a combination of several factors: a "sixth-year" election with a Democrat in the White House, a pro-Republican midterm turnout pattern, a wildly pro-Republican landscape for members of Congress (especially senators), and a strongly "wrong-track" public opinion profile reinforced by negative perceptions of the economy and the president.

The national House vote—the best measurement of overall political sentiment—gave Republicans a 6.1 percent margin of victory, a bit under the 2010 margin of 6.8 percent.

The composition of the electorate was very similar to 2010: 75 percent white (77 percent white in 2010, 72 percent in 2012); 37 percent sixty and over (32 percent in 2010, 25 percent in 2012); 12 percent thirty and under (12 percent in 2010, 19 percent in 2012). The party splits in various demographics also strongly resembled 2010; the better Republican numbers in pro-Democratic groups (i.e., 36 percent among Latinos in 2014, 38 percent in 2010, 27 percent in 2012) reinforces the impression that more conservative voters turned out across the board. (One startling improvement for Republicans, a surge from 26 percent in 2012 to 50 percent among Asian-Americans, is generally thought to reflect a questionable sample in one year or both.[6])

While the midterm turnout patterns were largely predictable, the results call into question the vaunted DSCC's Bannock Street Project, a $60 million investment in reshaping the midterm electorate via the voter targeting and contact techniques deployed so successfully by the Obama campaign in 2012.

But a postelection examination by the *New York Times'* Nate Cohn found significant evidence that Bannock Street did pay dividends: "The preliminary and qualified answer is that the Democratic field effort was probably a success. An analysis of precinct and county-level returns, supported by exit polls and limited voter file data, suggests that the turnout in key Senate battlegrounds was generally more favorable for Democrats than it was in 2010. When it wasn't, the Democratic turnout still seemed impressive when compared with the states where they did not make significant investments, like Virginia or Maryland."[7] Since turnout overall was at an estimated 36.6 percent, the lowest level since 1942, Cohn's findings would suggest that even more abysmal turnout might have occurred if Democrats had not invested heavily in GOTV efforts in states with close Senate races (with Republicans almost certainly stepping up their own GOTV program, especially with respect to early voting).

Like any winning party, Republicans sought to claim a policy mandate from the election. Exit polls did not, however, identify any particular public sentiment as critical, other than pessimism and hostility to Washington.[8] Although Democrats clearly suffered from being the sitting president's party at a time of high "wrong-track" sentiment, exit polls did not indicate a particularly high voter determination to admonish or "block" Barack Obama, at least outside the polarized ranks of self-identified Republicans (with 45 percent indicating Obama was not a factor one way or another in their congressional votes). Attitudes toward "GOP Leaders in Congress" were just as negative as those toward the president, and approval/disapproval ratings for the two parties were roughly even.

With partisan confrontations over executive powers quickly dominating Washington after the election, it's worth noting from the exit polls that those voters who did turn out marginally "trusted" the GOP over the president on relevant issues like immigration, though a majority of the same voters still supported a "path to citizenship" for undocumented immigrants.

The heavy early anti-Obamacare advertising by Republican candidates and pro-Republican outside groups noted in Chapter 3 did not significantly affect stable public opinion disapproving of the law (while also opposing its complete repeal).[9]

It should especially be noted that whereas the heavy drumbeat of ads advocating a minimum wage increase did not work electoral magic for Democrats, state-level ballot initiatives on the subject did extremely well. No less than four states that elected Republican senators on November 4 (Alaska, Arkansas, Nebraska, and South Dakota) also approved minimum wage increases by ballot initiative.[10]

Aside from the minimum wage initiatives, there were, as usual, a host of additional ballot measures. Two states, Oregon (by a comfortable 56–44 margin) and Alaska (more narrowly) joined Colorado and Washington as states legalizing the production, sale, and consumption of marijuana.[11] The District of Columbia passed a more limited initiative legalizing homegrown production and possession of marijuana but not its sale, though a Republican-controlled Congress might choose to interfere with enforcement of the new law.[12]

Personhood initiatives were defeated in Colorado (for a third time, though this time proponents tried the indirect route of defining zygotes as persons for purposes of criminal liability)[13] and in North Dakota. Right-to-lifers did win a ballot initiative in Tennessee that eliminated any state constitutional protections for abortion, which could become important in that state if *Roe v. Wade* is reversed.[14]

Aside from legalizing marijuana, Oregon voters decisively defeated an initiative to emulate Washington and

California in adopting a "top-two" election system with no party primaries.[15] Oregonians also turned back an initiative to require labeling of genetically modified foods by just 837 votes.[16]

In other environmentally related ballot initiatives, Alaskans banned mining practices that affected salmon.[17] And, as noted earlier, rural voters poured out in Maine to defeat an initiative aimed at preventing bear baiting, apparently deemed a precious hunting practice.[18]

Although this was the most expensive nonpresidential election ever, with $3.7 billion spent, the general consensus is that money was not crucial in the overall results. Democratic candidates and party committees outspent their Republican counterparts, with pro-Republican outside groups more than making up the difference. The authoritative Center for Responsive Politics, which tracks campaign spending, put it this way: "In terms of overall numbers, CRP projects Republicans will hold the advantage when it comes to money spent on this 2014 midterm election. When all is said and done, Team Red (all Republican candidates, parties, committees and conservative outside groups) will spend $1.75 billion on this election. Team Blue (all Democratic candidates, parties, committees and liberal outside groups) will spend a total of $1.64 billion—still a significant amount, but definitively less than the conservative side."[19]

As noted in Chapter 3, however, pro-Republican groups showed an impressive ability to pursue a division of labor, particularly between Karl Rove's American Crossroads cluster and the Koch brothers' family of groups. And a couple of high-profile progressive donors had less successful outings. Tom Steyer's $65 million investment via the Next Gen Climate Super PAC yielded three wins (Jeanne Shaheen and Gary Peters in Senate races and Tom Wolf in a gubernatorial race) and four losses (Mark Udall and Bruce Braley in Senate races and Mike Michaud and Charlie Crist in gubernatorial races).[20] The campaign finance advocacy Super PAC Mayday.us, headed by Lawrence Lessig and Mark McKinnon, spent $10 million and went zero-for-five in competitive races.[21]

As is often the case in midterm elections, there was much discussion of whether campaigns would be "nationalized." The general consensus was that 2014 was indeed "nationalized," a judgment retroactively confirmed by the relatively uniform results. This notion suggests that Republicans were effective in keeping the focus on Barack Obama, which thwarted the efforts of Democrats, especially in red states, to separate themselves from Obama or the national party—or for incumbents to make contests revolve around their own accomplishments.

But one can make a strong argument that the steady decline in ticket splitting in recent years,[22] combined with the ideological realignment of the two parties and the erosion of regional differences within the parties, has made "localized" campaigns, at least for Congress, an anachronism.

If issues, money, or "nationalization" were not crucial to the outcome, did any factors other than "the fundamentals" matter?

Clearly, as always, the quality of candidates and campaigns made a difference in some contests.

Perhaps it is unfair to blame Bruce Braley for the viral video of the candidate telling Texas trial lawyers they had an opportunity to block the "Iowa farmer" Chuck

Grassley from chairing the Senate Judiciary Committee. But it had a large impact on the course of the campaign, almost perfectly setting up Joni Ernst's homey general election campaign as the hog-castrating embodiment of Iowa values—and convincing national Republican donors and strategists that Iowa was winnable.

Maryland's shocking gubernatorial result was without question partially attributable to an uninspiring and over-confident campaign by Democratic nominee and Lt. Gov. Anthony Brown, who did nothing to address anger at a highly unpopular tax signed by his predecessor Martin O'Malley.[23]

And even in a victory, Mark Warner's stubborn determination to campaign in heavily Republican areas as a symbol of his bipartisanship instead of boosting Democratic turnout nearly cost him his Senate seat.[24]

Conversely the single biggest difference between the 2010 and 2016 Senate races in Colorado is that Cory Gardner and his campaign handled criticism of his record on reproductive rights much more smoothly this year than Ken Buck did four years ago. (It was also helpful that Colorado Republicans talked Buck into running for Gardner's open House seat instead of persisting in another Senate campaign.[25])

National Republicans were also very deft in offering high-life political talent to candidates in trouble, particularly Kansas Sen. Pat Roberts, whose entire campaign operation was taken over in a "rescue" operation.

Finally, it is difficult not to wonder if positive media coverage pressed a thumb to the scales for the GOP. As noted in Chapters 2 and 3, a widespread media narrative held that the Republican Party had finally acquired the discipline to rein in the Tea Party and avoid the kind of unfortunate candidates who had damaged the party's Senate prospects so noticeably in 2010 and 2012. This narrative arguably influenced media coverage of GOP general election candidates, giving short shrift to extremist positions and utterances because attention to them would have contradicted the cycle's overall "story line" of a Republican Party cleaning up its act and preparing to participate responsibly in governing after being chastened by its 2012 defeat and bad publicity surrounding the 2013 government shutdown. Thus, for example, a long series of Joni Ernst comments that were reminiscent of Sharron Angle's 2010 gaffes and Todd Akin and Richard Mourdock's 2012 abortion extremism were largely ignored amid constant commentary about her outstanding qualities as a candidate.

I do not suggest that mainstream media were "pro-Republican" in the sense of wanting GOP candidates to win or that party to govern. But there is a substantial recent history of "neutral" media being eager to marginalize extremist elements in either party by denying their influence and insisting on the equivalent determination of the two parties to seek the "political center," with the median voter serving as the North Star. It is largely a coincidence that the political commentariat got the outcome they had long predicted—a negative referendum on Obama benefiting a newly "pragmatic" Republican Party, setting up a climactic struggle in 2016 between a reinvigorated GOP and Hillary Clinton.

Chapter 5

Implications for the Future

As previous chapters have indicated, we are not in an era where one election necessarily follows from the previous one. We've now seen three consecutive "swings" in turn-out patterns and results that reinforce the "two electorates" hypothesis, suggesting a structural Republican advantage in midterms and a Democratic advantage in presidential elections. Since it emerged in 2008, the close alignment of the two parties with the segments of the electorate most likely (Republicans with their older white voter base) and least likely (Democrats with their younger and minority voter base) to participate in midterms, nobody's "broken serve" yet. It could happen in 2016, of course. One scary possibility for Democrats is that both high turnout in the "Obama coalition" of young and minority voters and the very high Democratic percentages in these demographic groups were a temporary phenomenon occur-ring only when Barack Obama was on the ballot. Indeed, that's an alternative explanation for the relatively strong Republican percentages among young and minority vot-ers in both Obama midterms. (The more likely explana-tion is that more conservative elements of the "Obama coalition" turn out in midterms.) If, on the other hand, the "Obama coalition" represents a trend rather than an aberration occurring in two unique elections, Democrats could begin the next cycle with the same kind of structural advantage Republicans enjoyed in 2014.

Changes in the electoral landscape for 2016 also reinforce the likelihood that turnout patterns will produce another metronomic swing back toward Democrats. The Senate landscape in 2016 is arguably as favorable to Democrats as the 2014 landscape was favorable to Republicans: twenty-four of the thirty-six seats up in 2016 are held by Republicans; seven are in states carried by Barack Obama twice; and five are in states carried by every Democratic presidential nominee since 1992 (see Figure 5).

Cumulative GOP House victories in 2010 and 2014 have made Republicans "overexposed" going into 2016.

Senate Landscape in 2016

● Dem Inc./Carried by Obama '12
◉ GOP Inc./Carried by Romney '12
◌ GOP Inc./Carried by Obama '12

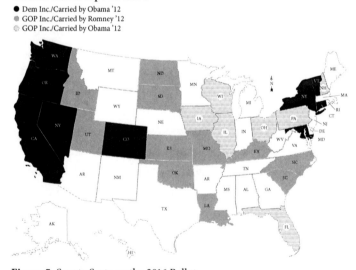

Figure 5. Senate Seats on the 2016 Ballot

There are now twenty-six Republicans occupying House districts carried by Obama in 2012 and only five Democrats in districts carried by Romney. As Kyle Kondik and Geoffrey Skelley of *Larry Sabato's Crystal Ball* noted after the dust had begun to settle from the midterm election, "Clearly, Republicans are now overextended in the House, and some of the seats they won this year—IA-1, NV-4, NY-24, to name a few—will be very hard to hold in the long run. But with Democrats needing to flip about 30 seats to take control of the chamber, the Republicans have built themselves a comfortable buffer."[1]

Only eleven governorships are up in 2016; Republicans might be favored to make small net gains with term-limited Democrats leaving office in Republican-trending West Virginia and Missouri.

Some analysts, notably *RealClearPolitics*' Sean Trende,[2] believe Barack Obama's low approval ratings were a more important factor in the 2014 results than the turnout and landscape factors and suggest Obama's relative unpopularity, if it persists (particularly alongside negative perceptions of the economy), could be a significant advantage for Republicans going into 2016.

Beyond Obama's approval ratings, political scientists point out two-term presidents are not often succeeded by nominees of their own party; Stevenson in 1952, Nixon in 1960, Ford in 1976, Gore in 2000, and McCain in 2008 all lost in an effort to succeed a two-term president. (Stevenson actually followed five straight Democratic victories.) On the other hand, Truman in 1948 and George H. W. Bush in 1988 broke this pattern; Al Gore in 2000 won the popular vote; and the Nixon and Ford losses were among the closest in US history. The sample set of post-two-term-president elections is too small and too ambiguous to provide much predictive value.

Aside from such "fundamentals" as economic trends (or voter perceptions of them) and the lame-duck Obama's approval ratings, the most important variable affecting the next cycle will be the presidential contest. And the initial positioning of the two parties with respect to the nominating process could not be much different.

If she chooses to run, Hillary Clinton could well become the strongest nonincumbent candidate for the nomination of either party since Richard Nixon (who was then vice-president) in 1960.

There have been four potential candidates who have talked seriously about challenging her. The earliest, former Montana governor Brian Schweitzer, already an unlikely challenger thanks to his positions on guns (he has long been a NRA favorite) and fracking (he has fought Bureau of Land Management regulations on fracking on public lands) damaged himself significantly when in a single 2014 interview he used language offensive to LGBT people and to women while hurling insults at former House Majority Leader Eric Cantor and Sen. Diane Feinstein.[3] His name is now rarely mentioned as a viable 2016 candidate.

The possible Clinton alternative who has done the most to prepare for a 2016 campaign is Maryland Gov. Martin O'Malley, who in the 2014 cycle paid the traditional entry fee to an Iowa Caucus bid by sending staff to help down-ballot Iowa candidates and speaking at local Democratic fundraisers.[4] (He performed similar chores on a smaller scale in the first primary state, New Hampshire.) Thought by many to be angling for a vice-presidential nomination and/or a future race, O'Malley saw his stock among Democratic and media elites take a dive when his designated successor, Lt. Gov. Anthony Brown, was upset on November 4, with a tax signed into law by the incumbent being most often cited as the culprit.[5]

Former Sen. Jim Webb of Virginia has not matched O'Malley's investments in early states but has become the first significant candidate in either party to form an exploratory committee.[6] Webb has attracted much interest among progressives looking for someone willing to attack Hillary Clinton's alleged hawkishness from the unassailable position of a veteran and a former secretary of the Navy.[7] But Webb's past service to the Reagan administration, and particularly his past passionate opposition to women serving in the military, makes him an unlikely figure to lead a left-bent insurgency against someone aiming to become the first woman to serve as president.[8] And Webb is famously allergic to fundraising.

Finally, there's independent (caucusing with Democrats) senator Bernie Sanders of Vermont, who as the only self-identified socialist in the Senate has something of a national following and seems quite serious about a race—probably as a Democrat but possibly as an independent—that would mainly be aimed at (to use a term often tellingly deployed by those hoping for a primary challenge to Clinton) "keeping Hillary honest."

The fact that even Democrats hoping and praying for a challenge to Clinton so often speak in terms of influencing rather than defeating her is not very encouraging to someone who would be expected to endure the brutality of the presidential campaign trail—and possibly the enmity of a Democratic president.

Short of a highly improbable bid by Sen. Elizabeth Warren (who has repeatedly expressed disinterest in the idea) or some revelation that changes all expectations (though it is hard to imagine what they might be for someone whose every step for decades has been reviewed by hostile researchers), Clinton's nomination is highly probable. You cannot say that about any potential Republican candidate.

Indeed, if Clinton is in the most dominant position within her party of any nonincumbent since 1960, a good case could be made that the GOP presidential field for 2016 is the most wide open since 1940.

As of this writing, the list of seriously "mentioned" 2016 candidates includes Senators Ted Cruz, Lindsay Graham, Rand Paul, Rob Portman, and Marco Rubio; former Senator Rick Santorum; Governors Chris Christie, Bobby Jindal, John Kasich, Mike Pence, and Scott Walker; former Governors Jeb Bush and Mike Huckabee; US Rep. Paul Ryan; political novice Ben Carson; hardy perennial "mentioned" Condoleezza Rice; and in some precincts, even former unsuccessful Senate candidate (and CEO) Carly Fiorina. And as if to underline the absence of any 2016 frontrunner, 2012 frontrunner and ultimate nominee Mitt Romney has indicated a strong interest in a comeback, and has led early polls in which he was listed as an option.[9]

Not all these candidates, of course, will actually run, and some could be culled from the race before voting begins (though it should be noted that in 2012 the only announced candidate who dropped out before the Iowa caucuses was Tim Pawlenty, who gambled and lost his entire campaign treasury on an unsuccessful bid to win the Iowa GOP's Ames straw poll).

The dynamics for the early emergence of a front-runner, however, are not good. There are multiple candidates who enjoy Republican establishment support, including access to robust financial resources: Chris Christie, Jeb Bush, and Marco Rubio. Even if one of them decides not to run, all three are doing poorly in early polling in Iowa, and all have taken ideological positions that are disliked by the conservative activists who tend to play a disproportionate role in the early Caucus and primary states. (Christie accepted the Affordable Care Act's Medicaid expansion in his state. Bush supports both an immigration "path to citizenship" and Common Core education standards. Rubio lead the bipartisan Senate "gang of eight" that drafted the comprehensive immigration legislation loathed by "the base.")

Another variable in the GOP contest will be the certainty of congressional conflict with Barack Obama. It will offer senators like Cruz, Graham, Paul, Portman, and Rubio opportunities to distinguish themselves in partisan warfare. But partisan warfare could also push perceptions of the entire field and of the party to the right, while creating competitive pressure for outspokenness, especially among the governors who do not get to lead filibusters or directly engage Democrats in Washington.

As of this writing, congressional Republicans seem to be struggling with themselves to avoid the dynamics that led them into the nearly disastrous government shutdown of 2013, as they search for a lever big enough to interfere with the president's executive action on immigration. Obama's initiative has enraged both "the base" and

conservative media figures and given even past supporters of comprehensive immigration reform an excuse to
unite with "amnesty" opponents in attacks on executive
"tyranny." But it is not clear where this path will lead, and
long-term Republican prospects may not be enhanced
by persistent and angry resistance to an initiative that is
initially drawing wildly positive reactions from Latinos,
per a November 20–22 poll by Latino Decisions, which
showed an astonishing 89 percent of Latino voters supporting Obama's initiative, including 81 percent of self-
identified independents and 76 percent of Republicans.
According to Matt Barreto, who oversaw the poll, "This is
the most unified we have ever seen Latino public opinion
on any issue."[10]

The authors of the famous 2013 RNC "autopsy report"
on the future of the Republican Party were already
alarmed at the positioning of the GOP coming out of
2012 and urged a change of course: "We are not a policy
committee, but among the steps Republicans take in the
Hispanic community and beyond, we must embrace and
champion comprehensive immigration reform. If we do
not, our Party's appeal will continue to shrink to its core
constituencies only."[11]

The "self-deportation" posture of the Romney campaign was bad enough; would a Republican Party moving
decisively to a position favoring mass *forced* deportations
be in real danger of long-term alienation of the fastest
growing demographic group in the country? Said the
"autopsy" report, "If Hispanic Americans perceive that a
GOP nominee or candidate does not want them in the
United States (i.e. self-deportation), they will not pay
attention to our next sentence."[12]

Aside from the perils associated with the immigration collision with Obama, another potential trap involves Supreme Court review of a lawsuit challenging the statutory authorization for Obamacare insurance purchasing subsidies in the thirty-six states that did not set up their own exchanges.[13] While a decision invalidating the subsidies might be expected to spur wild joy among conservatives happy to see the hated new "entitlement" in trouble, its immediate impact would probably be to hike insurance premiums for middle-class people—many of them Republican voters—mostly in the red states that refused to set up state exchanges.

And as James Surowiecki of *The New Yorker* has pointed out, this could cause serious dissension in the Republican ranks:

> The Republican hatred of Obamacare is so powerful, and Republican politicians' fear of being challenged from the right is so strong, that there will undoubtedly be states where governors and legislatures hold firm and basically tell citizens that they can't have, and shouldn't want, the free money that the federal government is offering them. (Something like this already happened, after all, when some states opted out of Obamacare's expansion of Medicaid, even though the federal government was going to pay almost all the costs.) But, given that this will wreck the individual market for health insurance in these states, that it will (unlike Medicaid) affect plenty of middle-class voters, and that Democrats will be able to point to states where the subsidies are still intact as obvious success stories, staying true to conservative principles is going to be a very hard political sell—even in truly red states.[14]

Republicans only have until June to figure out a common line on what to do in this situation—unless they want to gamble that the Supreme Court's acceptance of the subsidy case (which requires only four justices) is a false alarm. And this is just one of the issues on which maintaining unity and avoiding long-term political damage will not be easy, especially in the face of constant conflict with a president in a position to block or defy most of their demands. It will be ironic if their success in convincing the news media and a majority of swing voters that they are a disciplined party that has tamed its extremists during the 2014 campaign displays indiscipline and extremism almost immediately.

But Democrats, too, have some immediate challenges, beyond recalibrating the relationship of their depleted ranks in Congress to a (now officially) lame-duck president. The party has two urgent policy and messaging challenges, one domestic, one international: (1) to develop a post-Obama, post-Great Recession economic agenda that links growth to greater equality and real wage gains and resolves the party's ambivalent attitude toward the financial sector and (2) to forge a coherent Democratic foreign policy and national security posture amid the ruins of the liberal and conservative illusions of the last quarter century. Politically, Democrats must resist the "demography is destiny" temptation to wait for a durable majority coalition to emerge; it could take a long time. And even if they can hold their own at the federal level through metronomic alternating election victories, the erosion of Democratic strength at the state level—and with it both the ability to govern in the less gridlocked parts of American government and to build a political bench—could spell future trouble.

As the party of an activist public sector, Democrats have a special if not exclusive responsibility to figure out a way to overcome the paralysis that unstable majorities, divided government, and the use of obstructionist tactics now regularly produce in Washington. It is entirely possible that the solution ritualistically offered by "respectable" opinion leaders—bipartisanship—is simply impractical for the immediate future, not because politicians are selfish or "out of touch" but because they do indeed reflect fundamentally different constituencies holding fundamentally different views about government's role in national life, America's role in the world, and the need to accept or resist profound changes in our culture and family structure.

Indeed, both parties need to come to grips with the consequences of continued instability in power arrangements and whether it might be better to have *someone* in charge of the federal government, even if it is the "enemy," instead of lurching along from crisis to crisis with a choice between inaction and short-range impure "compromises" that sacrifice the best instincts of *both* parties and make consistent policymaking impossible.

Unfortunately for those who fantasize about a return to "bipartisanship" (a tradition that was largely the product of a completely archaic party system in which ideological coalitions frequently trumped party loyalty), the major political trends exhibited in 2014 lend themselves to a continued shift in emphasis from persuading "swing voters" to mobilizing "base voters." Aside from the availability of ever-more-sophisticated voter targeting and motivation techniques used by both parties, the decline in ticket splitting and true political independence means that it often makes more sense for a party to seek voters who already agree with its agenda than to try to woo undecided voters, who for the most part are undecided about whether or not to participate in elections at all.

Then there is the long-awaited displacement of that great standardizer of political messaging, the broadcast media ad (along with, of course, the continued marginalization of broadcast media news). Ben Smith of *BuzzFeed* sounded a messianic note in an announcement of his organization's new partnership with Facebook, but it's not as outlandish as it might initially sound:

> Facebook is on the cusp—and I suspect 2016 will be the year this becomes clear—of replacing television advertising as the place where American elections are fought and won. The vast new network of some 185 million Americans opens the possibility, for instance, of a congressional candidate gaining traction without the expense of television, and of an inexpensive new viral populism. The way people share will shape the outcome of the presidential election. Even during the 2014 midterms, which most Americans ignored, Facebook says it saw 43 million unique individuals engage in the political conversation. Now a rawly powerful video may reach far more voters in a few hours than a multimillion-dollar ad buy; and it will reach them from trusted sources—their friends—not via suspect, one-way channels.[15]

As Smith goes on to note, the emergence of e-mail has already revolutionized small-donor fundraising and campaign organizing. Social media have an even greater potential in political operations, ranging from voter persuasion and mobilization to measurement of public opinion. But a large part of what makes social media a vast new frontier in voter appeals is the capacity to customize communications to ever-more-refined target audiences, making standardized broadcast advertising clumsy and obsolete.

Perhaps technological change will lubricate enough creaky joints in the body politic to produce a shift in the current configurations of power. That's a more positive vision than the vain hope of a return to the sort of old-school "bipartisanship" that often meant old men cutting impure deals that betrayed everyone outside the quiet rooms they accessed with keys bequeathed by entrenched privilege. We may yet look back on the midterm elections of 2014 as a transition point from one political era to another, tarnished by apathy and cynicism but ultimately producing a general conviction that we cannot go on this way forever.

Acknowledgments

I would like to acknowledge the assistance of my friend and editor, Damon Linker of the University of Pennsylvania Press. Most of all I wish to thank my wife, Dawn Wilson, to whom this book is dedicated. Her timely, perfectionist help proved essential to getting it done and done right.

N o t e s

Chapter 1

1. US Bureau of Labor Statistics, "The Recession of 2007–2009," *BLS Spotlight on Statistics*, February 2012, http://www.bls.gov/spotlight/ 2012/recession/pdf/recession_bls_spotlight.pdf.

2. Geoffrey Skelley, "Senate Class Population Imbalance," *Sabato's Crystal Ball*, May 29, 2014, http://www.centerforpolitics.org/crystalball/ articles/senate-class-population-imbalance.

3. "Presidential Approval Ratings—Bill Clinton," *Gallup.com*, October 29–November 1, 1998, http://www.gallup.com/poll/116584/ presidential-approval-ratings-bill-clinton.aspx.

4. Patrick Mortiere, "Timeline of Botched ObamaCare Rollout," *The Hill*, November 15, 2013, http://thehill.com/blogs/blog-briefing-room/ news/190485-timeline-of-botched-implementation-of-obamacare.

5. "Gallup Daily—Obama Job Approval," *Gallup.com*, accessed December 1, 2014, http://www.gallup.com/poll/113980/Gallup-Daily -Obama-Job-Approval.aspx.

6. Charlie Cook, "A Historic Collapse," *Cook Political Report*, December 9, 2013, http://cookpolitical.com/story/6530.

7. Patrick Mortiere, "Timeline of Botched ObamaCare Rollout," *The Hill*, November 15, 2013, http://thehill.com/blogs/blog-briefing-room/ news/190485-timeline-of-botched-implementation-of-obamacare.

8. Ashley Parker, "Democrats Aim for a 2014 More Like 2012 and 2008," *New York Times*, February 6, 2014, http://www.nytimes.com/ 2014/02/07/us/politics/democrats-aim-to-make-2014-more-like-2012 -and-2008.html.

9. David Wasserman, "Introducing the 2014 Cook Political Report Partisan Voter Index," *Cook Political Report*, April 4, 2013, http://cookpolitical.com/story/5604.

10. David Wasserman, "December House Overview: GOP Back on Track to Gain Seats," *Cook Political Report*, December 12, 2013, http://cookpolitical.com/story/6543.

Chapter 2

1. Daniel Malloy, "David Perdue Takes U.S. Chamber Attack to TV with 'Amnesty' Spot," *Atlanta Journal-Constitution*, July 18, 2014, http://politics.blog.ajc.com/2014/07/18/david-perdue-takes-u-s-chamber-attack-to-tv-with-amnesty-spot.

2. Samantha Lachman, "GOP Senator Thad Cochran Is Facing Residency Questions in Competitive Primary," *Huffington Post*, May 5, 2014, http://www.huffingtonpost.com/2014/05/05/thad-cochran-senate-_n_5266685.html.

3. David Martosko, "'The Worst Race-Baiting Ads I've Ever Seen': Radio Ads in Mississippi Senate Race Accused Tea Party Candidate of Ku Klux Klan Links and Drove Black Democrats to Vote Against Him in a Republican Primary," *Mail Online*, June 27, 2014, http://www.dailymail.co.uk/news/article-2672565/The-worst-race-baiting-ads-Ive-seen-Radio-ads-Mississippi-senate-race-accused-tea-party-candidate-Ku-Klux-Klan-links-drove-black-Democrats-vote-against-REPUBLICAN-primary.html.

4. "Cochran Challenger Building Evidence towards Legal Action against Mississippi GOP Runoff Results," *CNN Politics*, July 7, 2014, http://politicalticker.blogs.cnn.com/2014/07/07/cochran-challenger-to-take-legal-action-against-mississippi-gop-runoff-results.

5. Sean Sullivan, "Pat Roberts Doesn't Have His Own Home in Kansas," *Washington Post*, February 7, 2014, http://www.washingtonpost.com/blogs/post-politics/wp/2014/02/07/pat-roberts-doesnt-have-his-own-home-in-kansas.

6. Sydney Lupkin, "Doctor-Turned-Politician Posted Gruesome Images to Facebook," *ABC News*, February 25, 2014, http://abcnews.go.com/Health/doctor-turned-politician-posted-gruesome-images-facebook/story?id=22654225.

7. Dermot Cole and Nathaniel Herz, "Sullivan Declares Victory in High-Stakes GOP Senate Primary," *Alaska Dispatch News*, August 20, 2014, http://www.adn.com/article/20140820/sullivan-declares-victory-high-stakes-gop-senate-primary.

8. Sean Sullivan, "Hanabusa Won't Challenge Outcome of Hawaii U.S. Senate Primary," *Washington Post*, August 20, 2014, http://www.washingtonpost.com/blogs/post-politics/wp/2014/08/20/hanabusa-wont-challenge-outcome-of-hawaii-u-s-senate-primary.

9. Tarini Parti, "Idaho's Mike Simpson Beats Club for Growth-Backed Bryan Smith," *Politico*, May 21, 2014, http://www.politico.com/story/2014/05/idaho-primary-results-mike-simpson-106928.html.

Chapter 3

1. "Obama Approval Ratings in Key States," *RealClearPolitics*, accessed December 1, 2014, http://www.realclearpolitics.com/epolls/2014/president/obama_job_approval_key_states.html.

2. "United States GDP Growth Rate 1947–2014," *Trading Economics*, accessed December 1, 2014, http://www.tradingeconomics.com/united-states/gdp-growth.

3. US Bureau of Labor Statistics, "Databases, Tables & Calculators by Subject," November 28, 2014, http://data.bls.gov/timeseries/CES0000000001?output_view=net_1mth.

4. Greg Giroux, "Obamacare Foes Run Nearly Half of Early Ads for Congress," *Bloomberg News*, March 13, 2014, http://www.bloomberg.com/news/2014-03-14/obamacare-foes-run-nearly-half-of-early-ads-for-congress.html.

5. Rebecca Kaplan, "Leon Panetta Criticizes Obama for Iraq Withdrawal," *CBS News*, October 2, 2014, http://www.cbsnews.com/news/leon-panetta-criticizes-obama-for-iraq-withdrawal.

6. See "Problems and Priorities," *PollingReport.com*, accessed December 1, 2014, http://www.pollingreport.com/prioriti.htm.

7. Jon Swaine, "Scott Brown Rolls Immigrants, Isis and Ebola into Unholy Trinity of Terror," *The Guardian*, November 3, 2014, http://www.theguardian.com/us-news/2014/nov/03/scott-brown-immigrants-isis-ebola-terror-new-hampshire.

8. "Executive Order 13658—Establishing a Minimum Wage for Contractors," *Federal Register* vol. 79, no. 34, February 20, 2014, http://www.gpo.gov/fdsys/pkg/FR-2014-02-20/pdf/2014-03805.pdf, 9851–9854.

9. Jonathan Topaz, "Mitt Romney: Raise the Minimum Wage," *Politico*, May 9, 2014, http://www.politico.com/story/2014/05/mitt-romney-minimum-wage-106524.html.

10. "Most See Inequality Growing, but Partisans Differ Over Solutions," *Pew Research Center for the People & the Press*, January 23, 2014, http://www.people-press.org/2014/01/23/most-see-inequality-growing-but-partisans-differ-over-solutions.

11. William Saletan, "Social Outcasts: Republican Candidates Are Retreating from Debates on Abortion, Gay Marriage, and Contraception," *Slate*, September 30, 2014, http://www.slate.com/articles/news_and_politics/politics/2014/09/republican_candidates_are_avoiding_social_issues_gop_politicians_don_t_want.html.

12. Lynn Bartels, "Cory Gardner's New Ad: 'I Believe the Pill Ought to Be Available over the Counter,'" *Denver Post*, September 2, 2014, http://blogs.denverpost.com/thespot/2014/09/02/cory-gardner-birth-control-senate/112040.

13. James Hohmann, "Bruce Braley, Joni Ernst Tear into Each Other," *Politico*, September 2014, http://www.politico.com/story/2014/09/bruce-braley-joni-ernst-debate-2014-iowa-senate-elections-111409_Page2.html#ixzz3EiPe1eBe.

14. Phillip Rucker and Robert Costa, "Battle for the Senate: How the GOP Did It," *Washington Post*, November 5, 2014, http://www.washingtonpost.com/politics/battle-for-the-senate-how-the-gop-did-it/2014/11/04/a8df6f7a-62c7-11e4-bb14-4cfea1e742d5_story.html.

15. See "Begich Releases Most Inflammatory Attack on Sullivan Yet," *AmandaCoyne*, August 29, 2014, http://amandacoyne.com/politics/begich-releases-most-inflammatory-attack-on-sullivan-yet.

16. Nate Silver, "Senate Update: Alaska, a Frontier for Bad Polling," *FiveThirtyEight*, September 14, 2014, http://fivethirtyeight.com/datalab/senate-update-alaska-a-frontier-for-bad-polling.

17. Phillip Rucker, "In Alaska's Remote Villages, Begich Quietly Built an Advantage on the Ground," *Washington Post*, October 4, 2014, http://www.washingtonpost.com/national/in-alaskas-remote-villages-begich-quietly-built-an-advantage-on-the-ground/2014/10/04/219c6756-4a9f-11e4-891d-713f052086a0_story.html.

18. Charlie Cook, "The Arkansas Race Is Not Over Yet," *National Journal*, May 15, 2014, http://www.nationaljournal.com/the-cook-report/the-arkansas-race-is-not-over-yet-20140515.

19. Philip Bump, "A State-By-State Look at the Record Black Turnout in 2012," *The Wire*, May 9, 2013, http://www.thewire.com/politics/2013/05/black-turnout-2012-state-by-state-maps/65053.

20. Andra Gillespie and Tyson King-Meadows, "Black Turnout & the 2014 Midterms," *Joint Center for Political and Economic Studies*, October 29, 2014, http://jointcenter.org/sites/default/files/Joint Center 2014 Black Turnout 10-29-14_0.pdf, 5–6.

21. "Arkansas Senate—Cotton vs. Pryor," *RealClearPolitics*, accessed December 1, 2014, http://www.realclearpolitics.com/epolls/2014/senate/ar/arkansas_senate_cotton_vs_pryor-4049.html#polls.

22. Dylan Scott, "The Strategy Dems Are Betting Will Save Mark Udall—and the Senate," *Talking Points Memo*, October 15, 2014, http://talkingpointsmemo.com/dc/mark-udall-2014-is-like-michael-bennet-2010.

23. Joey Bunch, "Colorado Prepares for All-Mail Election under New Statewide Rules," *Denver Post*, October 24, 2014, http://www.denverpost.com/news/ci_24375485/colorado-prepares-all-mail-election-under-new-statewide.

24. John Bresnahan and Manu Raju, "David Perdue: 'I Spent Most of My Career' Outsourcing," *Politico*, October 3, 2014, http://www.politico.com/story/2014/10/david-perdue-georgia-senate-race-2014-111589.html.

25. Chris Joyner, "Perdue 'Proud' of Outsourcing Past, Blames Washington for Jobs Lost," *Atlanta Journal-Constitution*, October 6, 2014, http://www.ajc.com/news/news/state-regional-govt-politics/perdue-proud-of-outsourcing-past-blames-washington/nhcsk.

26. Nate Cohn, "Early Voting Numbers Look Good for Democrats," *New York Times*, October 31, 2014, http://www.nytimes.com/2014/10/31/upshot/early-voting-election-results-hold-good-news-for-democrats.html?abt=0002&abg=1.

27. "Dem Rep. Bruce Braley: Chuck Grassley 'An Iowa Farmer Who Never Went to Law School,'" *RealClearPolitics*, March 25, 2014, http://www.realclearpolitics.com/video/2014/03/25/bruce_braley_chuck_grassley_is_just_an_iowa_farmer_who_never_went_to_law_school.html.

Ed Kilgore

28. "Squeal," YouTube video, 0:30, posted by "Joni Ernst," March 24, 2014, https://www.youtube.com/watch?v=p9Y24MFOfFU.

29. Philip Rucker, "In Iowa, a Dispute Over Neighbor's Chickens Threatens Braley's Senate Bid," *Washington Post*, August 7, 2014, http://www.washingtonpost.com/politics/in-iowa-a-dispute-over-neighbors-chickens-threatens-braleys-senate-bid/2014/08/07/4ae3d5e2-1e47-11e4-ae54-0cfe1f974f8a_story.html.

30. Dave Weigel, "An Update on America's Dumbest Senate Race," *Slate*, August 13, 2014, http://www.slate.com/blogs/weigel/2014/08/13/an_update_on_america_s_dumbest_senate_race.html.

31. David Corn, "Secret Tape: McConnell and Aides Weighed Using Judd's Mental Health and Religion as Political Ammo," *Mother Jones*, April 9, 2013, http://www.motherjones.com/politics/2013/04/mitch-mcconnell-ashley-judd-secret-tape-senate.

32. "Grimes Surges Ahead of McConnell in Poll," *Courier-Journal*, October 10, 2014, http://www.courier-journal.com/story/news/politics/elections/kentucky/2014/10/06/mcconnell-grimes-bluegrass-poll-due-tonight/16798721.

33. Joseph Gerth, "Democratic Group Halts Ads in Ky. Senate Race," *Courier-Journal*, October 15, 2014, http://www.courier-journal.com/story/news/politics/elections/kentucky/2014/10/14/grimes-loses-democratic-senatorial-tv-ads/17262333.

34. Dana Bash, "DCCC Back on the Air in Kentucky," *CNN Politics*, October 22, 2014, http://www.cnn.com/2014/10/22/politics/dscc-back-in-kentucky.

35. Perry Bacon Jr., "In Debate, Grimes Again Refuses to Answer Obama Vote Question," *NBC News*, October 14, 2014, http://www.nbcnews.com/politics/first-read/debate-grimes-again-refuses-answer-obama-vote-question-n225201.

36. Jason Easley, "Bill Maher Rips Cowardly Democrats Who Are Throwing President Obama under the Bus," *Politicus USA*, November 1, 2014, http://www.politicususa.com/2014/11/01/bill-maher-cowardly-democrats-throwing-obama-bus.html.

37. Sam Trende, "Why Is Mary Landrieu in So Much Trouble?" *RealClearPolitics*, October 23, 2014, http://www.realclearpolitics.com/articles/2014/10/23/why_is_mary_landrieu_in_so_much_trouble_124397.html.

98

38. Julia O'Donoghue, "Judge Throws Out Suit Challenging Mary Landrieu's Residency," *Times-Picayune*, September 5, 2014, http://www.nola.com/politics/index.ssf/2014/09/landrieu_residency_court_case.html.

39. "Louisiana Senate—Cassidy vs. Landrieu," *RealClearPolitics*, November 4, 2014, http://www.realclearpolitics.com/epolls/2014/senate/la/louisiana_senate_cassidy_vs_landrieu-3670.html.

40. "New Hampshire Senate—Brown vs. Shaheen," *RealClearPolitics*, accessed December 1, 2014, http://www.realclearpolitics.com/epolls/2014/senate/nh/new_hampshire_senate_brown_vs_shaheen-3894.html#polls.

41. Matea Gold, "In N.C., Conservative Donor Art Pope Sits at Heart of Government He Helped Transform," *Washington Post*, July 19, 2014, http://www.washingtonpost.com/politics/in-nc-conservative-donor-art-pope-sits-at-heart-of-government-he-helped-transform/2014/07/19/eece18ec-0d22-11e4-b8e5-d0de80767fc2_story.html.

42. Dave Helling and Brad Cooper, "Democrat Chad Taylor's Exit Shakes up U.S. Senate Race in Kansas," *Kansas City Star*, September 3, 2014, http://www.kansascity.com/news/government-politics/article1447419.html.

43. "Results of *SurveyUSA* Election Poll #21712," *SurveyUSA*, October 6, 2014, http://www.surveyusa.com/client/PollReport.aspx?g=459ff79a-7e55-4e15-acd5-f86f146ae3a7.

44. Bob Mercer, "Rounds Signed 2005 EB-5 Recruitment Letter," *Aberdeen News*, October 11, 2014, http://www.aberdeennews.com/news/local/rounds-signed-eb—recruitment-letter/article_15fc60e1-01a5-5c69-9345-2ca53121206e.html.

45. Mark Halperin, "Exclusive: Senate Democrats Flooding South Dakota Airwaves," *Bloomberg News*, October 8, 2014, http://www.bloomberg.com/politics/articles/2014-10-08/exclusive-senate-democrats-flooding-south-dakota-airwaves.

46. Thomas Beaumont, "GOP in Uphill Battle in Michigan US Senate Fight," *Associated Press*, September 9, 2014, http://bigstory.ap.org/article/gop-uphill-battle-michigan-us-senate-fight.

47. Ibid.

48. Mark Z. Barabak, "Stalker Charge Turns Oregon Senate Race into Fight on Gender Politics," *Los Angeles Times*, June 2, 2014, http://www.latimes.com/nation/politics/politicsnow/la-pn-oregon-senate-wehby-20140602-story.html#page=1.

49. John Bresnahan, "Second Harassment Accusation vs. Monica Wehby," *Politico*, May 19, 2014, http://www.politico.com/story/2014/05/monica-wehby-harassment-106854.html.

50. Andrew Kaczynski, "Oregon Doctor GOP Senate Candidate's Health Plan Plagiarized from Karl Rove Group's Survey," *BuzzFeed*, September 16, 2014, http://www.buzzfeed.com/andrewkaczynski/doctor-oregon-gop-senate-candidates-health-plan-plagiarized.

51. Andrew Kaczynski, "Monica Wehby Blames Second Plagiarized Health Care Plan On Former Staffer," *Politico*, October 9, 2014, http://www.buzzfeed.com/andrewkaczynski/monica-wehby-blames-second-plagiarized-health-care-plan-on-f.

52. Andrew Kaczynski, "Oregon Doctor GOP Senate Candidate's Health Plan Plagiarized from Karl Rove Group's Survey," *BuzzFeed*, September 16, 2014, http://www.buzzfeed.com/andrewkaczynski/doctor-oregon-gop-senate-candidates-health-plan-plagiarized.

53. "Virginia Senate—Gillespie vs. Warner," *RealClearPolitics*, accessed December 1, 2014, http://www.realclearpolitics.com/epolls/2014/senate/va/virginia_senate_gillespie_vs_warner-4255.html#polls.

54. "2014 House Race Ratings for January 6, 2014," *Cook Political Report*, January 6, 2014, http://cookpolitical.com/house/charts/race-ratings/6572.

55. "2010 Competitive House Race Chart," *Cook Political Report*, January 7, 2010, http://cookpolitical.com/archive/chart/house/race-ratings/2010-01-07_12-37-26.

56. Scott Bland, "Spending in Florida's Special Election Is Only the Beginning," *National Journal*, March 10, 2014, http://www.nationaljournal.com/daily/spending-in-florida-s-special-election-is-only-the-beginning-20140310.

57. Michael E. Miller, "Alex Sink Loses Special Election, Dealing Blow to Democrats and Obamacare," *Miami New Times*, March 12, 2014, http://blogs.miaminewtimes.com/riptide/2014/03/alex_sink_loses_special_electi.php.

58. Micah Cohen, "Popular Governors, and Prospects for 2016," *FiveThirtyEight*, May 28, 2013, http://fivethirtyeight.blogs.nytimes.com/2013/05/28/popular-governors-and-prospects-for-2016/?smid=tw-share&_r=0.

59. Adam C. Smith, Mary Ellen Klas, Marc Caputo, and Kathleen McGrory, "Gov. Rick Scott, Charlie Crist Start Final Push; Scott

Adds $12.8 Million to Campaign," *Tampa Bay Times*, November 1, 2014, http://www.tampabay.com/news/politics/stateroundup/gov-rick-scott-in-tampa-bay-as-reports-show-he-gave-his-campaign-128/2204705.

60. Daniel Malloy, "AJC Poll: Governor's Race in Virtual Tie, David Perdue Has Slight Lead for Senate," *Atlanta Journal-Constitution*, September 12, 2014, http://politics.blog.ajc.com/2014/09/12/ajc-poll-governors-race-in-virtual-tie-david-perdue-has-slight-lead.

61. Micah Cohen, "Popular Governors, and Prospects for 2016," *FiveThirtyEight*, May 28, 2013, http://fivethirtyeight.blogs.nytimes.com/2013/05/28/popular-governors-and-prospects-for-2016/?smid=tw-share&_r=0.

62. Sophia Tareen, "Illinois Pension Law Signed into Law by Governor Quinn," *Huffington Post*, December 5, 2013, http://www.huffingtonpost.com/2013/12/05/illinois-pension-law-sign_n_4393614.html.

63. Greg Hinz, "Quinn Doubles Down on Tax Hike Gamble," *Crain's Chicago Business*, March 26, 2014, 2014, http://www.chicagobusiness.com/article/20140326/BLOGS02/140329819/quinn-doubles-down-on-tax-hike-gamble.

64. Eric Pianin, "Brownback Feeling Big Political Backlash to Tax Cuts in Kansas," *Fiscal Times*, July 16, 2014, http://www.thefiscaltimes.com/Articles/2014/07/16/Brownback-Feeling-Big-Political-Backlash-Tax-Cuts-Kansas.

65. Brad Cooper, "Reagonomics Guru Arthur Laffer Touts Brownback Tax Plan at Capitol," *Kansas City Star*, January 19, 2012, http://www.kansascity.com/news/local/article300536/Reagonomics-guru-Arthur-Laffer-touts-Brownback-tax-plan-at-Capitol.html.

66. Micah Cohen, "Popular Governors, and Prospects for 2016," *FiveThirtyEight*, May 28, 2013, http://fivethirtyeight.blogs.nytimes.com/2013/05/28/popular-governors-and-prospects-for-2016/?smid=tw-share&_r=0.

67. "Kansas Governor—Brownback vs. Davis," *RealClearPolitics*, 2014, accessed December 1, 2014, http://www.realclearpolitics.com/epolls/2014/governor/ks/kansas_governor_brownback_vs_davis-4146.html#polls.

68. Sean Sullivan, "Three Reasons the Paul Davis Strip Club Story Could Hurt Him in Kansas," *Washington Post*, September 22, 2014, http://www.washingtonpost.com/blogs/post-politics/wp/2014/09/22/three-reasons-the-paul-davis-strip-club-story-could-hurt-him-in-kansas.

69. "Charlie Baker for Governor," *Boston Globe*, October 26, 2014, http://www.bostonglobe.com/opinion/editorials/2014/10/26/charlie -baker-for-governor/r4Yymw55jVr20D53EhUIkK/story.html.

70. Tara Culp-Ressler, "Maine Governor Vetoes Medicaid Expansion for the Third Time," *ThinkProgress*, April 10, 2014, http:// thinkprogress.org/health/2014/04/10/3425353/maine-governor-medicaid.

71. Chris Cillizza, "Why Scott Walker Won the Wisconsin Recall," *Washington Post*, June 5, 2012, http://www.washingtonpost.com/blogs/ the-fix/post/why-scott-walker-won-the-wisconsin-recall/2012/06/05/ gJQAfbOGHV_blog.html.

72. "The Battle for Congress," *Vox*, accessed November 3, 2014, http://www.vox.com/a/election-2014-forecast.

73. "2014 General Congressional Vote," *RealClearPolitics*, accessed December 1, 2014, http://www.realclearpolitics.com/epolls/other/generic _congressional_vote-2170.html.

74. Larry J. Sabato, Kyle Kondik, and Geoffrey Skelley, "The Crystals Ball's Final 2014 Picks," *Sabato's Crystal Ball*, November 3, 2014, http://www.centerforpolitics.org/crystalball/articles/the-crystal-balls -final-2014-picks.

75. Nate Silver, "The Polls Might Be Skewed against Democrats—or Republicans," *FiveThirtyEight*, October 15, 2014, http://fivethirtyeight .com/features/the-polls-might-be-skewed-against-democrats-or -republicans.

Chapter 4

1. Michael P. McDonald, "Early Voting Pulling into the Station," *HuffPost Pollster*, November 2, 2014, http://www.huffingtonpost.com/ michael-p-mcdonald/early-voting-pulling-into_b_6091452.html.

2. For a sense of what this felt like from the other side of the partisan fence, see "Midterms Liveblog #4: Florida Looks Good Early, Runoff in Georgia?" *Daily Kos*, November 4, 2014, http://www.dailykos .com/story/2014/11/04/1341427/-Midterms-liveblog-4-XXX?detail=hide.

3. Joe Jordan, "'Dang Straight' It Was Rep. Lee Terry's Fatal Flaw," *Nebraska Watchdog*, November 7, 2014, http://watchdog.org/182002/ dang-straight-terry.

4. Jake Sherman, "How to Blow an Easy GOP Win," *Politico*, October 19, 2014, http://www.politico.com/story/2014/10/2014-florida-elections-steve-southerland-gwen-graham-112020.html.

5. Nate Silver, "The Polls Were Skewed toward Democrats," *FiveThirtyEight*, November 5, 2014, http://fivethirtyeight.com/features/the-polls-were-skewed-toward-democrats.

6. Karthick Ramakrishnan, "What 2014 Does—and Does Not—Tell Us about Asian Americans' Voting," *Washington Post*, November 13, 2014, http://www.washingtonpost.com/blogs/monkey-cage/wp/2014/11/13/what-2014-does-and-does-not-tell-us-about-asian-americans-voting.

7. Nate Cohn, "For Democrats, Turnout Efforts Look Successful (Though Not Elections)," *New York Times*, November 14, 2014, http://www.nytimes.com/2014/11/15/upshot/evaluating-the-success-of-democratic-get-out-the-vote-efforts.html?_r=0&abt=0002&abg=1.

8. "House: Full Results," *CNN.com*, November 20, 2014, http://www.cnn.com/election/2014/results/race/house#exit-polls.

9. Liz Hamel, Jamie Firth, Bianca DiJulio, and Mollyann Brodie, "Kaiser Health Tracking Poll: October 2014," *Kaiser Family Foundation*, October 21, 2014, http://kff.org/health-reform/poll-finding/kaiser-health-tracking-poll-october-2014.

10. National Employment Law Project, "Campaigns," *Raising the Minimum Wage*, November 2014, http://www.raisetheminimumwage.com/pages/campaigns.

11. Jonathan L. Fischer, "Marijuana Legalization Passes in Oregon, Alaska, D.C.," *Slate*, November 3, 2014, http://www.slate.com/blogs/the_slatest/2014/11/05/marijuana_legalization_oregon_alaska_and_d_c_pass_ballot_measures.html.

12. "Washington D.C. Marijuana Legalization, Initiative 71," *Ballotpedia*, November 2014, http://ballotpedia.org/Washington_D.C._Marijuana_Legalization,_Initiative_71_%28November_2014%29.

13. Amanda Marcotte, "Colorado Says No to Personhood for the Third Time," *Slate*, November 4, 2014, http://www.slate.com/blogs/xx_factor/2014/11/04/personhood_goes_down_in_colorado_voters_say_no_to_amendment_67.html.

14. Amanda Marcotte, "Why 'Personhood' Lost, but an Anti-Abortion Tennessee Initiative Won," *RH Reality Check*, November 6, 2014, http://rhrealitycheck.org/article/2014/11/06/personhood-lost-anti-abortion-tennessee-initiative-won.

15. "Oregon Open Primary Initiative, Measure 90," *Ballotpedia*, November 2014, http://ballotpedia.org/Oregon_Open_Primary_Initiative, _Measure_90_(2014).

16. "Oregon GMO Measure 92 Headed for Recount," *KGW*, November 24, 2014, http://www.kgw.com/story/news/politics/2014/11/24/oregon-gmo-measure-92-headed-for-recount/70068394.

17. State of Alaska Division of Elections, "Alaska Ballot Measure No. 4—12BBAY, An Act Providing for Protection of Bristol Bay Wild Salmon and Waters Within or Flowing Into the Existing 1972 Bristol Bay Fisheries Reserve," accessed December 1, 2014, http://www.elections .alaska.gov/doc/bml/BM4-12BBay-ballot-language.pdf.

18. "Maine Voters Rejecting Bear-Baiting, Hunting Restrictions," *USA Today*, November 5, 2014, http://www.usatoday.com/story/news/politics/elections/2014/11/05/bear-baiting-hunting-restrictions-leading -in-maine/18520643.

19. Center for Responsive Politics, "Overall Spending Inches Up in 2014: Megadonors Equip Outside Groups to Capture a Bigger Share of the Pie," *OpenSecrets*, October 29, 2014, http://www.opensecrets.org/news/2014/10/overall-spending-inches-up-in-2014-megadonors-equip -outside-groups-to-capture-a-bigger-share-of-the-pie.

20. Timothy Cama, "Half-Victory for Climate Billionaire," *The Hill Online*, November 5, 2014, http://thehill.com/policy/energy -environment/222979-elections-a-half-victory-for-climate-billionaire.

21. Byron Tau and Kenneth P. Vogel, "How to Waste $10 Million," *Politico*, November 6, 2014, http://www.politico.com/story/2014/11/2014 -elections-mayday-pac-larry-lessig-112617.html.

22. See Phillip Bump, "The Remarkable Recent Decline of Split-Ticket Voting," *Washington Post*, November 10, 2014, http://www .washingtonpost.com/blogs/the-fix/wp/2014/11/10/polarization-and-the -decline-of-split-districts.

23. Brentin Mock, "Was the Shocking Outcome of Maryland's Gubernatorial Race about Rain, or Something Else?" *Grist*, November 7, 2014, http://grist.org/politics/was-the-shocking-outcome-of-marylands -gubernatorial-race-about-rain-or-something-else.

24. Jenna Portnoy and Rachel Weiner, "On His Way to a Slim Victory in a Changing Va., Warner May Have Wooed Wrong Voters," *Washington Post*, November 5, 2014, http://www.washingtonpost.com/local/virginia-politics/with-warner-ahead-vote-certification-begins-in-tight

-virginia-senate-race/2014/11/05/4ffcff0c-6507-11e4-9fdc-d43b053ecb4d
_story.html.

25. Lynn Bartels and Kurtis Lee, "Cory Gardner to Challenge Mark Udall, Ken Buck to Seek Gardner's Seat," *Denver Post*, February 26, 2014, http://www.denverpost.com/news/ci_25233265/u-s-rep -cory-gardner-enter-u-s.

Chapter 5

1. Kyle Kondik and Geoffrey Skelley, "14 from '14: Quick Takes on the Midterm," *Sabato's Crystal Ball*, November 13, 2014, http://www .centerforpolitics.org/crystalball/articles/14-from-14-quick-takes-on-the -midterm.

2. Sean Trende, "Midterm Demographics Didn't Sink the Democrats," *RealClearPolitics*, November 19, 2014, http://www.realclearpolitics .com/articles/2014/11/19/midterm_demographics_didnt_sink_the _democrats_124701.html.

3. Mike Dennison, "Schweitzer in Firestorm over Cantor 'Gaydar' Remark, Feinstein Insult," *Missoulian*, June 20, 2014, http://missoulian .com/news/local/schweitzer-in-firestorm-over-cantor-gaydar-remark -feinstein-insult/article_a55ed0e4-f7e6-11e3-bde3-001a4bcf887a.html.

4. Ken Thomas and Thomas Beaumont, "Despite Clinton: O'Malley in Iowa amid 2016 Talk," *Associated Press*, July 26, 2014, http:// bigstory.ap.org/article/despite-clinton-omalley-iowa-amid-2016-talk.

5. Matthew Yglesias, "How Did Democrats Lose Maryland? Meet the Rain Tax," *Vox*, November 6, 2014, http://www.vox.com/2014/11/6/ 7159239/rain-tax.

6. Reid J. Epstein, "Jim Webb Forms Exploratory Committee for 2016 Presidential Bid," *Wall Street Journal*, November 20, 2014, http:// blogs.wsj.com/washwire/2014/11/20/jim-webb-forms-exploratory -committee-for-2016-presidential-bid.

7. William Greider, "Hillary's Nightmare?" *The Nation*, October 22, 2014, http://www.thenation.com/article/184617/hillarys-nightmare.

8. Michael D. Shear and Tim Craig, "Va. Senate Race Goes Negative on 1979 Essay," *Washington Post*, September 14, 2006, http:// www.washingtonpost.com/wp-dyn/content/article/2006/09/13/ AR2006091302301.html.

9. Matt Viser, "Mitt Romney Crafting a Rationale for 2016 Run," *Boston Globe*, January 14, 2015. https://www.bostonglobe.com/news/politics/2015/01/14/private-mitt-romney-starting-outline-rationale-for-third-presidential-campaign/QoYvBak5C4tvaxpezuNbLM/story.html

10. "New Poll Results: National Poll Finds Overwhelming Support for Executive Action on Immigration," *Latino Decisions*, November 24, 2014, http://www.latinodecisions.com/blog/2014/11/24/new-poll-results-national-poll-finds-overwhelming-support-for-executive-action-on-immigration.

11. Republican National Committee, "Growth & Opportunity Project," March 18, 2013, http://goproject.gop.com/rnc_growth_opportunity_book_2013.pdf, 8.

12. Ibid.

13. Lyle Denniston, "Court to Rule on Health Care Subsidies," *SCOTUS Blog*, November 7, 2014, http://www.scotusblog.com/2014/11/court-to-rule-on-health-care-subsidies.

14. James Surowiecki, "On Obamacare, the G.O.P. Lays a Trap for Itself," *The New Yorker*, November 18, 2014, http://www.newyorker.com/news/daily-comment/obamacare-g-o-p-lays-trap.

15. Ben Smith, "The Facebook Election," *BuzzFeed News*, November 9, 2014, http://www.buzzfeed.com/bensmith/the-facebook-election#.bjLxVAorl.

CPSIA information can be obtained at www.ICGtesting.com
Printed in the USA
BVOW07*1932280115

385423BV00001B/1/P